Richard Deacon's Microwave Oven Cookbook

Published by H. P. Books, 4058 N. 14th Ave., Tucson, Arizona 85705
Co-Publisher, Thermador, 5119 District Blvd., Los Angeles, California 90040

Recipes developed and tested by Mable Hoffman
Assisted by Lorine Craft
All food photography by George de Gennaro
Editor, Mary M. Powers
Layout and design—Joyce Reese & Cornell Morton
Illustrations—Cornell Morton

ISBN Number 0-912656-20-4 (Hardcover)
ISBN Number 0-912656-21-2 (Paperback)
Library of Congress Catalog Card Number 73-93782
H. P. Book Number 16

foreword

Microwave Ovens are truly an appliance of the future. While their greatest advantage has been the speed with which they cook food, this same speed has added an energy conserving quality to the oven. This is a most attractive feature.

There are over two million ovens in use today, and there are many fine creative cooks who are enjoying the speedy performance of microwaves and the ease with which culinary perfection is achieved.

Microwave Ovens come in a variety of styles, sizes and combinations. Some have infra-red browning elements: some will accept some metal food containers as will Thermador Microwave Ovens in which these recipes have been tested. Interiors are designed with a number of finishes varying from inexpensive plastic to sparkling stainless steel. There is a type and price for each potential user. And the number of users continues to increase every day.

This book has been compiled mainly for the users of Thermador Microwave Equipment and recipes were tested in the Thermatronic. However, we are pleased to share these recipes with users of other makes of equipment who want to expand their own collection of microwave recipes.

Let the expertise of the professionals who developed and tested these recipes be your bridge to the convenient and exciting world of microwave cooking. It is an adventure you'll enjoy.

to all microwave oven user

I have a couple of strong suggestions that are mentioned elsewhere in this book but can bear repeating.

1. Before you use any make of microwave oven read the instructions thoroughly and particularly the section which refers to the use of metal. While some makes of ovens will tolerate metal in limited amounts others will not accept it at all. *Be Sure You Follow the Instructions of the Make You Own. Not doing so may cause damage to component parts and be an expensive mistake.*

2. Always undercook the food and add time as you need it. There are many factors that can affect cooking time slightly, such as the temperature of food at starting time or cooking a quantity of food that differs from that stated in the recipe. You can always add time, but overcooking may spoil the recipe.

Remember these suggestions and enjoy the fun of Microwave Cooking.

Richard Deacon

table of contents

About This Cookbook

This book has been divided by recipe categories instead of by meals. These recipe categories will allow you to plan a meal according to your own likes. Basic recipes are given and from these many different complete meals can be prepared.

The recipes have been tested and retested many times in Thermador's Thermatronic Oven to insure the accuracy of the cooking times. At first, please follow the suggested timings. If your taste preference is for softer vegetables, well done meat etc., recipe times can be increased slightly.

Get acquainted with the Thermatronic™ Oven and Cookbook, then adapt your own recipes by following similar ones in this book. Use the same size and shape of utensils indicated and cook covered or uncovered as specified.

Microwave Cooking

Time is the keynote in microwave cooking—not temperature. The time will vary with the volume of the food, its density and starting temperature. Unless otherwise specified, the ingredients in these recipes were at room temperature at preparation time.

It is always best to undercook, test for doneness, as you would in conventional cooking, and add seconds of time, if needed.

Selecting Proper Cooking Utensils

The most suitable cooking utensils will transmit microwaves and remain cool. Many other utensils will either absorb or reflect microwaves and thus interfere with cooking time, cause uneven cooking of food, or may be damaged. One of the nice features of the Thermatronic Oven is that you may cook in some types of serving dishes, so that there are no pots or pans to clean. With foods that take a long period of time to cook, it is recommended that oven or heat proof dishes be used, as there is considerable heat transfer from the food to the cooking utensil. Always use oven proof dishes when using the browning element.

Glass and China

This category includes glass, ceramic and china. Dishes with a metal trim (gold or silver) should not be used, as the metal trim may be damaged. Some paints and glazes used on various glass items contain metalic substances, and these dishes should not be used in the microwave oven. If in doubt, check with the dish manufacturer.

Oven Proof Glass

In this category are dishes which are designed for conventional oven usage (electric or gas). This type of dish is fine for use in the microwave oven. However, the manufacturer's instructions should be consulted before using it under the infrared element.

Broiler Proof Dishes

These are dishes that are made for use under a conventional broiler and they can be used under the infrared element.

Corning Ware®

All Corning products can be used except those with some metal in the construction. *Do not use Centura® Dinnerware and Cook-n-Serve Covers and the Corelle® closed handle cups.*

Paper

This includes towels, dishes, napkins, cartons, freezer wrap, waxed paper, etc. When reheating food you may use paper dishes. Plastic coated paper dishes are recommended to retard the absorption of juices. Paper towels placed under the food are good absorbers for moisture and/or grease. Paper towels placed over the food will reduce spatter.

DO NOT USE THE INFRARED BROWNING ELEMENT WITH PAPER

Plastics

Plastic wraps, dishes, bags, semi-rigid freezer containers, etc., are suitable for use in the microwave oven. Plastics must be used with caution. Use only for heating food, not cooking. Avoid plastic or plastic combinations that are not heat proof, transfer of the heat from the food may distort the container.

Some plastics absorb enough energy to cause charring, (Melamine Ware is an example of this type of plastic). This type of plasticware quickly becomes too hot to handle. We do not recommend this type for use in the microwave cooking.

DO NOT USE THE INFRARED BROWNING ELEMENT WITH PLASTIC PRODUCTS

Cooking Pouches

Cooking bags designed to withstand boiling, freezing and oven heat may be used according to the manufacturer's instructions. However, DO NOT use the metal twist ties for closing the bag, use string or rubber band.

Boil-in-a-bag pouches work very well, but they must be slit before cooking to allow steam to escape (see section on Convenience Foods).

DO NOT USE THE INFRARED BROWNING ELEMENT WITH COOKING POUCHES

Plastic wrap will play a very important role in the use of your microwave oven. Note that plastic wrap is used in many recipes. By the use of film covers you can shorten cooking times, obtain more even heat distribution in foods and reduce surface moisture evaporation. Use care in removing the film cover from the dish to avoid steam burns.

Straw

This type of basket can be used for the short time it takes to heat rolls, etc.

Wood

Wooden bowls or boards are not recommended for cooking in the microwave, as they dry out and may split or crack.

Metal

In general, we do not recommend using metal utensils for cooking, because metal containers are not compatible with microwave cooking. Microwaves are reflected by metal and therefore can reach the food only from the top of the container.

There are, however, instances when metal can be selectively used with good results. They are:

1. Aluminum foil can be used to slow down the cooking rate for a portion of a food item, such as the wings of a whole chicken, or turkey. When doing this, be certain the foil is not touching the walls or other metal parts of the oven.
2. Metal skewers, clamps, etc. if there is a larger amount of food in proportion to the metal.
3. TV dinners and convenience foods, if the containers are no higher than ⅞ inch deep. If the container is deeper than ⅞ inch, the food should be transferred to another container for heating to get the best results. Leaving the food in the container will not harm the oven. See section on Convenience Foods for detailed instructions.

If your microwave oven is not a Thermador, follow the manufacturer's instruction for the use of metal.

DO NOT HEAT CANNED FOODS IN THE CAN

Bonded Adhesive Handles

Some cups, mugs, and casserole covers have handles attached with glue. The handles may come off if these dishes are used in the microwave oven.

Lacquer Ware

If lacquer ware becomes heated, it may crack or become discolored.

When to Use What Containers

The recipes in this book specify the kind of utensils to be used. There are a few general rules to follow.

Reheating

When reheating food at serving time the non-metallic china may be used as well as the original cooking dish.

Food with less moisture content such as bread or rolls may be heated on paper plates, napkins or towels. Paper towels are used to cover many meats to keep the fats from spattering on the oven walls. Let towels keep your oven clean.

Size and Shape of Cooking Equipment

Size and shape of cooking equipment is important. Follow the instructions in the recipes. If a 3-quart, shallow casserole is called for, it is important that this size and shape be used in order to produce ideal results for that particular recipe.

Use a 4-quart casserole when that size is listed in a recipe, otherwise the food could boil over. The size and shape of dishes specified has been determined by the total volume of the food and the type of cooking job to be done.

Arrangement and Re-arrangement of Food

Instructions given in the recipes will provide the best results. Since food cooked by microwaves cooks from the outside, in, always place the thick parts of the food to the outside of the dish. It is important to re-arrange food, too, so that the food originally in the inside area of the dish, will be placed at the outer edge of the dish during part of the cooking time.

Some recipes also recommend turning the dish for more even cooking.

Stirring

Stirring is required in some recipes to prevent the outside edges from overcooking while the inside remains uncooked. You must stir some foods to obtain even heat distribution.

When it is necessary to stir food, remove the food from the oven. (You may need to use hot pads if the heat of the food has transferred to the dish.) When lifting the cover, tilt it away from you to avoid receiving a steam burn.

If you elect to leave the casserole in the oven, remove the cover as described and stir the food. Replace the cover. Close the door and timer starts again. By operating the oven in this manner you can stop the oven, stir the food and still have accurate timing. The timer advances only when the door is closed.

Standing Time Before Serving

Since food continues to cook after being removed from the oven, a standing or waiting period is needed before serving. It is very important to cover a roast or fowl with foil and let stand for 10 to 20 minutes after cooking. Inner temperature of the food rises during this standing time because of heat transfer.

Keep standing time in mind when planning meal serving time.

Don't stir food at the end of the cooking time. Let the food stand covered to continue cooking after it is taken from the oven.

Infrared Browning Element

The infrared browning element is designed to be used only for browning, not for cooking. It will provide the "finished" look to foods which have cooked so quickly they have not had time to brown naturally. There are many times you will use and enjoy the browning element.

There are two shelf positions. When the browning element is being used, it is best to have the shelf in the upper position providing the height of the food permits. The closer the food is to the browning element, the faster browning will be accomplished.

For regular cooking, leave the shelf in the lower position unless the recipe states otherwise. Recipes specify when to use a pre-heated browning element and state suggested browning times.

Defrosting of Foods

Before discussing defrosting, let us discuss packaging of meat for the freezer.

Ground Meat

It is best to form meat patties, make meat balls or meat loaves before freezing the ground meat. If this is not practical for you, form the ground meat into a flat circle, wrap in freezer paper and seal the package with freezer tape. An oblong package of ground meat could be starting to cook at the corners before the center is starting to defrost. This uneven defrosting won't matter, however, if you are defrosting and browning meat for a casserole or a "One-Dish Meal."

Wrap other meats in freezer paper and seal with freezer tape. Meat should be kept packaged for part of the defrosting time. As the meat defrosts it will be enveloped in a warm blanket of air and defrost more evenly and quickly.

Since ice absorbs very little microwave energy, use alternate cooking and standing times when defrosting. The standing times allows heat build-up on the exterior to spread toward the center of the food and prevents overcooking of the outside of meat, fish, poultry and casseroles. The size of the food determines the number of thaw cycles necessary.

Large items such as roasts and poultry should have thawing periods of 2 to 3 minutes with 5 minutes rest periods.

Once the outside of the meat feels warm and is thawed, thawing periods should be reduced to 30 seconds or 1 minute.

It is always more convenient to have the meat defrost overnight in the refrigerator. When this is not possible, it can be defrosted as described above.

Frozen casseroles may be defrosted by using this interruption procedure. After the food is defrosted, stir and cook as required.

Prepared frozen foods may be heated while still frozen.

Appetizer Meat Balls

1 egg, beaten slightly
⅓ cup milk
⅓ cup fine dry bread crumbs
1 tablespoon instant minced onion
1 teaspoon salt
1 teaspoon sugar
¼ teaspoon allspice
1 pound lean ground meat

Combine ingredients; form into 1-inch balls. Place on wire rack in 7½ x 12-inch baking dish. Cook by microwave 6 minutes, turning meat balls over once. Raise shelf. Turn on infrared browning element. Brown for 3 to 5 minutes. Makes about 25 meat balls.

Stuffed Mushrooms

4 slices bacon, diced
¼ cup minced onion
2 tablespoons minced green pepper
½ teaspoon salt
½ teaspoon Worcestershire sauce
1 (3-ounce) package cream cheese
1 pound fresh small mushrooms
½ cup soft bread crumbs
1 tablespoon butter or margarine

Combine bacon, onion, and green pepper in 4-cup measure. Cover with paper towel and cook by microwave for 4 minutes, stirring once. Remove from microwave; pour off fat. Mix in salt, Worcestershire and cream cheese. Wash and dry mushrooms. Remove stems. Chop stems and add to bacon mixture. Fill mushrooms. In 2-cup measure, heat bread crumbs and butter in microwave for 1 minute; stir until well mixed. Press buttered crumbs on top of stuffed mushrooms. Place half the mushrooms in 6 x 10-inch baking dish, filling side up. Add ¼ cup hot water to baking dish and cook 2 minutes. Repeat with remaining mushrooms. Makes about 50.

Opposite page. Appetizers from top; Cheese Puffs, page 17; Stuffed Mushrooms, page 15; Bacon Wrapped Water Chestnuts, page 17.

Hot Bacon - Bean Dip

1 (16-ounce) can red kidney beans, drained
3 slices bacon, diced
1 tablespoon chopped green pepper
1 teaspoon instant minced onion
½ teaspoon salt
¼ teaspoon garlic salt
⅛ teaspoon pepper
Dash hot pepper sauce
1 cup dairy sour cream

Mash beans. Cook bacon in 1½-quart casserole by microwave for 4 minutes. Pour off fat. Stir in beans, green pepper, onion, salt, garlic salt, pepper and hot sauce. Cook, covered, by microwave for 3 minutes. Stir in sour cream. Serve with corn chips. Makes about 2 cups.

"Meatzza" Pizza

1 pound lean ground beef
½ cup seasoned bread crumbs
½ teaspoon salt
⅛ teaspoon pepper
1 small can evaporated milk (5½-ounce)
1 (15-ounce) can pizza sauce
1 garlic clove, crushed
½ teaspoon oregano
1 cup shredded cheddar cheese
1 cup shredded jack cheese
1 (4-ounce) jar sliced mushrooms, drained
Sausage, salami, ripe olives (optional)

Mix beef, bread crumbs, salt, pepper and milk until well blended. Divide mixture into 2 equal parts. Press into two 9-inch pie plates to form a crust. Cook each meat crust 3 minutes by microwave. Combine sauce and garlic; bring to a boil. Pour sauce over crusts then sprinkle with oregano. Sprinkle cheeses over mixture and top. Add sausage, salami or ripe olives if desired. Brown pizza with shelf in upper position, under infrared browning unit 5 minutes. Remove from microwave and let stand 5 minutes. Cut into bite size pieces.

Bacon Wrapped Water Chestnuts

1 (8½-ounce) can water chestnuts, drained
8 slices bacon, cut in half
¼ cup soy sauce
½ teaspoon ground ginger
½ teaspoon garlic salt

Wrap each water chestnut in half slice of bacon. Secure with toothpick. Combine remaining ingredients. Pour over bacon-wrapped water chestnuts; refrigerate for several hours. Drain, reserving marinade. Place on rack in 7½ x 12-inch baking dish. Cover with paper towel. Cook 2 minutes by microwave; turn dish and cook another 2 minutes. Turn again and cook 2 minutes. Serve hot. Makes 16.

Cheese Puffs

3 green onions, finely chopped
1 cup grated cheddar cheese
½ cup mayonnaise
24 toast rounds

Combine green onions with cheese and mayonnaise. Spread on toast rounds. Heat half the rounds in 8¼-inch shallow baking dish by microwave for 1 minute 15 seconds or until bubbly. Turn baking dish once during cooking. Repeat with remaining puffs. Serve hot. Makes 24 appetizers.

Party Mix

2 cups shredded rice or wheat cereal
1 cup toasted oat cereal
1 cup stick pretzels
1 cup peanuts
1 tablespoon Worcestershire sauce
¼ cup melted butter or margarine
1 teaspoon garlic salt
1 teaspoon chili powder

In 2½-quart baking dish, combine cereals, pretzels and peanuts. Mix Worcestershire sauce, butter, garlic salt and chili powder. Pour over cereal mixture; mix well. Cook by microwave 6 minutes, stirring several times. Makes about 6 cups.

Beef Teriyakis

1 pound sirloin beef
¾ cup soy sauce
¼ cup dark brown sugar
1 small clove garlic, crushed
1 teaspoon dehydrated onion flakes
2 tablespoons lemon juice
1 teaspoon ground ginger
Wooden skewers

With a sharp knife cut meat into 1-inch cubes. Combine remaining ingredients; pour over beef cubes and let stand 1 hour at room temperature or in the refrigerator several hours. Thread 3 cubes of meat on 5-inch wooden skewers. Place 4 skewers on ovenproof platter. Cook 2 minutes, turn skewers over and cook 1 minute. Serve as an appetizer. Makes 8 servings.

Richard's Vegetable Dip

2 (4½-ounce) trimmed Brie cheese
1 (8-ounce) package cream cheese
1 (2-inch square) of sharp cheddar cheese slice
Brandy to taste
1 package walnuts (chopped)
1 bowl of celery, carrots and cauliflower

Put all the cheeses in 1½-quart bowl. Melt by microwave, stirring often. Add brandy to taste and beat. Fold in the walnuts. Refrigerate overnight in a covered container. Place in dip bowl with platter of fresh crisp vegetable sticks.

TIPS: Rotate position of baking dishes:
For quick and even cooking, remember to rotate dishes at least once while cooking by microwave.

Hot Cocoa

¼ cup sugar
¼ cup unsweetened cocoa powder
1 cup water
3 cups milk

In 1½-quart bowl, mix sugar with cocoa and water. Heat by microwave for 1½ minutes, stirring several times. Add milk and heat about 3 minutes or until piping hot, but not boiling. Makes 5 to 6 servings.

Mexican Chocolate

2 cups milk
¼ teaspoon ground cinnamon
2 ounces sweet cooking chocolate, chopped
2 teaspoons instant coffee
¼ cup whipped cream or whipped topping
2 teaspoons sugar, optional

In 4-cup measure, heat milk and cinnamon by microwave about 4 minutes. Stir in chocolate and coffee; heat 30 seconds. Beat with rotary beater until frothy. Whip cream with sugar or use whipped topping. Pour hot chocolate into mugs; top with whipped cream or topping. Makes 2 servings.

Hot Wine Cranberry Punch

1 pint cranberry juice cocktail
1 cup water
¾ cup sugar
2 sticks cinnamon
6 whole cloves
1 (⅘-quart) bottle burgundy wine
1 lemon, sliced

In 3-quart bowl, combine cranberry juice with water, sugar, cinnamon and cloves. Cover and heat by microwave for 10 minutes. Strain. Pour strained cranberry mixture into 3-quart bowl with wine and lemon. Heat by microwave for 5 minutes or until piping hot. Makes 12 to 15 punch cups.

Mulled Cider

1 quart cider
¼ cup brown sugar
1 stick whole cinnamon
3 whole cloves
Orange slices

In 2-quart baking dish, heat cider with sugar, cinnamon and cloves by microwave for 6 minutes. Strain and serve hot. Garnish with orange slices. Makes 4 servings.

Opposite page, Soup and Sandwiches; Minestrone Soup, page 22; Ham Stuffed Rolls, page 27.

Minestrone Soup

5 cups hot water
1 pound beef shanks or stew meat
1 small onion, diced
¼ teaspoon pepper
½ teaspoon basil
½ cup diced carrots
1 (1-pound) can tomatoes
½ cup uncooked spaghetti, broken into 1-inch pieces
2 zucchini, sliced
1 (16-ounce) can kidney beans, drained
1 cup shredded cabbage
1 teaspoon salt
Grated parmesan or romano cheese

In 4-quart casserole, pour water over meat; add onion, pepper and basil. Cover; cook by microwave 25 minutes, or until meat is tender, turning meat at least one time. Remove meat from bone; cut into small pieces. Add meat to soup broth, along with carrots and tomatoes; cover and cook by microwave for 8 minutes. Stir in spaghetti, zucchini, beans, cabbage and salt. Cover and cook another 10 minutes, stirring once. Let stand, covered, several minutes. Sprinkle with cheese. Makes 6 servings.

Oyster Stew

¼ cup butter or margarine
10 ounces shelled oysters, not drained
1 teaspoon Worcestershire sauce
1 teaspoon horseradish
1 teaspoon salt
½ teaspoon seasoned salt
4 cups milk

In 3-quart casserole, melt butter by microwave. Add undrained oysters. Cook for 2 minutes, stir and cook another minute. Mix in Worcestershire, horseradish, salt and seasoned salt. Pour in milk, cover and cook 5 minutes or until mixture is just below boiling point. Let stand several minutes. Makes 4 or 5 servings.

Curried Chicken Soup

1 (10¾-ounce) can cream of chicken soup, undiluted
1 soup-can milk
½ cup light cream
1 teaspoon curry powder
1 small apple, peeled and grated
1 teaspoon lemon juice
1 tablespoon chopped chives

In 2-quart bowl, combine all ingredients except chives. Cover and cook by microwave for 5 minutes, stirring several times. Garnish with chives. Makes 4 servings.

Quick Burger Soup

½ pound lean ground beef
¼ teaspoon salt
1 teaspoon instant minced dry onion
1 (10½-ounce) can vegetable beef soup
1 cup water
1 (8-ounce) can tomato sauce

In 2-quart bowl, cook beef 3 minutes by microwave, stirring once to break up chunks of meat. Pour off excess fat. Add salt, onion, soup, water and tomato sauce. Cook by microwave 4 minutes. Serve with toasted buns. Makes 4 servings.

Tomato Consomme

2½ cups tomato juice
1 (10½-ounce) can condensed consomme
¼ teaspoon seasoned salt
¼ teaspoon crumbled basil
¼ teaspoon sugar
4 lemon slices
8 whole cloves

Mix tomato juice with consomme, seasoned salt, basil and sugar in 1½-quart bowl. Stud lemon slices with cloves. Add to soup. Heat by microwave for 6 minutes. Makes 4 to 5 servings.

Main-Dish Chowder

1 onion, chopped
4 slices bacon, cut into small pieces
1 (1-pound) can potatoes, drained and cubed
1 (16-ounce) can cream style corn
1 (16-ounce) can whole kernel corn, not drained
1 (10¾-ounce) can cream of chicken soup
½ teaspoon Worcestershire sauce
1 teaspoon seasoned salt
¼ teaspoon pepper
2 cups milk
1 cup grated sharp cheddar cheese
chopped parsley

In 4-quart mixing bowl, cover and cook onion and chopped bacon by microwave for 6 minutes or until onion is soft. Drain fat except one tablespoon. Add potatoes, whole kernel corn, cream corn, soup, Worcestershire, seasoned salt, pepper and milk. Cook by microwave for 6 minutes. Stir in cheese; cook for 1 minute. Sprinkle with chopped parsley. Makes 6 servings.

New England Clam Chowder

2 (7½-ounce each) cans minced clams
or about 15 small fresh clams
2 slices bacon, diced
1 onion, diced
3 medium potatoes, peeled and diced
¼ cup butter or margarine
¼ cup flour
2 cups milk
½ teaspoon salt
⅛ teaspoon pepper

Drain canned clams, reserving liquid. If using fresh clams, cut into small pieces. Place bacon, onion and potatoes in 3-quart casserole. Add clam liquid and water to make 2 cups. Cover and cook by microwave 12 minutes. Remove from microwave. Melt butter in 2-cup measure. Stir in flour. Pour into potato mixture; mix well. Add milk, salt, pepper and clams. Cook another 5 minutes by microwave. Makes 6 servings.

Cream of Chicken Soup

6 tablespoons butter or margarine
⅓ cup flour
2 cups milk
2 cups chicken broth or bouillon
½ teaspoon seasoned salt
1 cup finely chopped cooked chicken

In 2½-quart bowl, melt butter by microwave. Stir in flour, then milk, broth, and seasoned salt. Cook by microwave for 6 minutes, stirring often. Add chicken; cook 1 minute. Makes 4 to 6 servings.

French Onion Soup

3 onions, thinly sliced
¼ cup butter or margarine
4 cups beef broth or bouillon
1 teaspoon Worcestershire sauce
½ teaspoon salt
5 or 6 slices French bread, toasted
grated Parmesan cheese

In covered 2½-quart casserole, cook onions and butter by microwave for 10 minutes. Stir in broth, Worcestershire and salt. Cover and cook another 5 minutes. Spoon into heat proof soup bowls. Sprinkle toast with cheese. Float on top of soup. Heat by microwave for 30 seconds. Makes 5 or 6 servings.

Irish Country Soup

1 (10¾-ounce) can cream of potato soup
1 (8-ounce) package frozen green peas with cream sauce
1 chicken bouillon cube
2 cups milk

Combine soup, peas, bouillon and milk in deep 1½-quart bowl. Heat by microwave 8 to 10 minutes or until bubbly hot, stirring often. Pour into blender. Blend until peas are broken up into small pieces. Makes 4 servings.

Split Pea Soup

1 cooked ham shank
2½ quarts water
1 teaspoon salt
¼ teaspoon pepper
1 small onion, chopped
1 stalk celery, chopped
1 carrot, peeled and chopped
1 pound dried split green peas

In 4-quart casserole, cover ham with water. Add salt, pepper, onion, celery, carrot and peas. Cover and cook by microwave 25 minutes. Remove ham shank from casserole; cut off any bits of ham. Add pieces of ham to sou · broth. Cook, covered, for another 30 minutes or until peas are soft. Thicken with flour, if desired. Makes 6 to 8 servings. (For smoother mixture, puree mixture in blender before serving.)

Bayou Soup

1 pound frozen or fresh cooked shrimp
1 (6-ounce) package frozen King Crab meat
1 can (10¾-ounce) condensed chicken broth
1 cup water
2 tablespoons freeze-dried shallot
1 whole bay leaf
½ teaspoon salt
¼ teaspoon dried basil leaves
¼ teaspoon tabasco sauce
1⅔ cups whole tomatoes and juice
1½ cups celery sliced
1 cup green pepper diced
1 cup carrots thinly sliced
1 cup zucchini thinly sliced
2 tablespoons lemon juice

Defrost shrimp and crab meat in package for 1 minute by microwave. Let stand for 2 minutes. Defrost by microwave for another minute. Set aside. Place chicken broth, water, shallot, bay leaf, salt, basil leaves, and tabasco sauce in a 4-quart bowl. Bring to a boil by microwave. Add tomatoes, celery, green pepper, carrots and zucchini. Cook covered for 8 minutes. Uncover, add shrimp and crab meat, then cook for 6 minutes. Served with garlic bread, this soup can be a main dish for 4.

Ham Stuffed Rolls

2 cups finely chopped cooked ham
2 hard cooked eggs, finely chopped
2 tablespoons minced green onion
2 tablespoons minced green pepper
1 teaspoon prepared mustard
1 tablespoon pickle relish
½ cup mayonnaise
4 large or 6 medium French rolls
½ cup shredded cheddar cheese

Combine ham with eggs, onion, pepper, mustard, relish and mayonnaise. Cut off top of rolls—scoop out; fill with ham mixture. Sprinkle with cheese. Place in 7½ x 12-inch baking dish. Heat by microwave 2 minutes. Turn dish; heat 1 additional minute. Makes 4 to 6 sandwiches.

Dill Cheese Loaf

2 cups pancake mix
1 tablespoon sugar
1 tablespoon instant minced onion
1 teaspoon dill weed
1 cup buttermilk or sour milk
1 egg
1 tablespoon melted butter or margarine
1 cup grated Swiss or Monterey Jack Cheese

Line bottom of 8 x 4-inch loaf-shaped baking dish with waxed paper. In mixing bowl, combine ingredients except cheese. Blend at low speed with mixer; beat 2 minutes at medium speed. Stir in cheese. Pour into baking dish. Cook by microwave for 8 minutes, turning dish a quarter turn every 2 minutes. Raise shelf. Brown under infrared browning element for 1 minute; turn and brown another minute. Let stand several minutes before serving. Makes 6 servings.

Open-face Veal Scaloppine Sandwiches

4 small frozen veal patties
2 tablespoons flour
1 tablespoon butter or margarine
1 tablespoon salad oil
1 (3-ounce) can sliced mushrooms, drained
2 tablespoons white wine
⅓ cup chicken broth
Salt and pepper
4 slices toasted French Bread

Partially thaw veal patties; coat with flour. Pour butter and oil in 7½ x 12-inch baking dish. Add meat. Cook by microwave 2 minutes, turning dish once. Turn veal over. Stir in mushrooms, wine, and broth. Cook 1 to 1½ minutes longer. Sprinkle with salt and pepper. Serve over toasted French Bread. Makes 4 open-face sandwiches.

Microwave Reuben Sandwich

4 slices pumpernickel or dark rye bread
¼ cup thousand island salad dressing
2 slices Swiss cheese
¼ cup sauerkraut, drained
Thin slices cooked corned beef

Spread bread with salad dressing. Top two slices of bread with slice of cheese, then sauerkraut and several thin slices of corned beef. Top with remaining two slices of bread. Heat by microwave for 45 seconds or until cheese melts. Makes 2 servings.

Hot Fish Stick Sandwich

8 breaded, ready to serve fish sticks
2 hamburger buns, split and toasted
¼ cup mayonnaise
2 tablespoons pickle relish
1 tablespoon finely chopped onion
½ teaspoon prepared mustard
⅛ teaspoon salt

Thaw fish sticks, if frozen. Arrange 2 fish sticks on each half of toasted bun. In 7½ x 12-inch dish, heat by microwave 2 or 3 minutes or until piping hot. In the meantime, combine mayonnaise with relish, onion, mustard and salt. Spoon sauce over each fish stick. Makes 4 open-face sandwiches.

Monte Cristo Sandwich

3 eggs
¼ teaspoon salt
1 teaspoon sugar
¼ cup milk
6 slices bread
Mayonnaise
Sliced chicken or turkey (3-ounce)
Sliced cheese
Sliced ham
4 tablespoons butter or mayonnaise

Beat eggs with salt, sugar and milk. Cut crusts off bread. Spread bread with mayonnaise. Make 3-decker sandwich starting with bread, then chicken, another slice of bread, sliced ham and cheese, another slice of bread. Insert toothpicks to hold together; cut into half. Dip each into egg mixture, turn sandwich over to coat all sides. Heat butter in 10 x 6-inch baking dish by microwave for 2 minutes. Place sandwiches in baking dish with melted butter. Spoon butter over top of bread. Cook by microwave 2 minutes. Turn sandwiches. Cook other side 3 minutes. Makes 2 sandwiches.

Hot Fudge Sauce

2 ounces unsweetened chocolate
⅔ cup evaporated milk
1 cup sugar
2 tablespoons butter or margarine
½ teaspoon vanilla
⅛ teaspoon salt

In 1½-quart bowl, melt chocolate by microwave. Combine with milk and sugar. Cook by microwave for 4 minutes, stirring often. Mix in butter, vanilla and salt. Beat with rotary beater until smooth. Serve over ice cream, cream puffs or plain cake. Makes about 1½ cups sauce.

Fresno Fruit Sauce

½ cup raisins
½ cup water
¼ cup currant jelly
½ cup orange juice
¼ cup brown sugar
1 tablespoon cornstarch
⅛ teaspoon allspice

In 4-cup measure, combine raisins with water, jelly and orange juice. Heat by microwave for 3 minutes or until jelly melts, stirring once. Mix sugar, cornstarch and allspice. Stir into raisin mixture. Cook by microwave for 1½ minutes, stirring every 30 seconds. Serve with baked ham, pork chops, or duck. Makes 1½ cups.

TIPS: Melt butter:
Melt 2 tablespoons butter in 15 seconds; ¼ cup in 30 seconds in glass measuring cup.

Opposite page.
Sauces from top in small pitcher; Fresno Fruit Sauce, page 31; Sweet Sour Sauce, page 35; (lower right) Creole Sauce, page 33; (lower left) Lemon Filling, page 33.

sauces & toppings

Barbecue Sauce

1 (8-ounce) can tomato sauce
¼ cup vinegar
2 tablespoons brown sugar
1 teaspoon prepared mustard
1 tablespoon Worcestershire sauce
1 tablespoon instant minced onion
¼ teaspoon salt
⅛ teaspoon liquid smoke

In 4-cup measure combine all ingredients. Cover with plastic wrap and cook by microwave for 5 minutes, stirring once. Let stand several minutes. Serve with ribs, chicken, chops, hamburger. Makes 1¼ cups.

Bordelaise Sauce

3 tablespoons butter or margarine
1 tablespoon minced onion
3 tablespoons flour
1 cup beef broth or bouillon
2 tablespoons red wine
1 tablespoon lemon juice
½ teaspoon dried tarragon, crushed
1 teaspoon finely chopped parsley
⅛ teaspoon brown sauce for gravy

In 4-cup measure, melt butter with onion by microwave. Stir in flour. Cook by microwave for 1 minute, stirring once. Pour in broth, wine, lemon juice, tarragon and parsley. Cook by microwave 3 minutes, stirring once every minute. Add bottled sauce. Makes about 1¼ cups. Serve with broiled steak or roast beef.

TIPS: Melt chocolate:
Use glass measuring cup to melt chocolate; 2-ounce unsweetened chocolate melts in 1½ to 2 minutes.

Creole Sauce

½ cup chopped onion
¼ cup chopped green pepper
¼ cup chopped celery
2 tablespoons butter or margarine
1 fresh tomato, peeled and chopped
1 (8-ounce) can tomato sauce
1 (3-ounce) can mushrooms, not drained
¼ teaspoon salt
⅛ teaspoon garlic powder

In 2-quart bowl, combine onion, pepper, celery and butter. Cook, covered for 4 minutes. Stir in remaining ingredients. Cover and cook another 5 minutes. Serve over cooked fish or vegetables. Makes 2½ cups.

Lemon Filling

¾ cup sugar
2 tablespoons cornstarch
¾ cup water
¼ cup lemon juice
½ teaspoon grated lemon peel
2 egg yolks, beaten slightly
2 tablespoons butter or margarine

In 4-cup measure or deep mixing bowl, mix sugar with cornstarch. Gradually add water. Stir in lemon juice and peel. Cook by microwave for 3 minutes or until mixture becomes translucent, stirring every 30 seconds. Add part of mixture to eggs; then return to measuring cup. Cook 1 minute, stirring once. Add butter. Cool several minutes. Use as filling for 8 or 9-inch cake.

TIPS: Measure butter or margarine by cutting the stick:
1 stick equals ½ cup or 8 tablespoons. ½ stick equals ¼ cup. ¼ stick equals 2 tablespoons. 2 sticks equals 1 cup butter.

Gravy

½ cup drippings (fat and juices from meat)
½ cup flour
4 cups liquid (broth, juices or water)
Salt and pepper
Bottled brown sauce for gravy (optional)

Pour drippings in 7½ x 12-inch baking dish or 3-quart casserole. Stir in flour. Cook by microwave for 1 minute, stirring once. Pour in liquid, stirring until well blended. Cook by microwave 4 to 5 minutes or until thick, stirring several times. Season with salt and pepper. Add a few drops of bottled sauce for a deeper brown color, if desired. Makes about 1 quart gravy.

Browned Lemon Butter

¼ cup butter or margarine
1 tablespoon lemon juice
Dash Worcestershire sauce

In 9-inch pie plate, heat butter on top shelf with infrared browning unit for 7 minutes or until it begins to turn golden. Cool slightly; stir in lemon juice and Worcestershire. Serve over cooked vegetables or fish.

TIPS: Cream sauces:
Save time by making cream sauces by microwave; stir several times for a smooth product.

Sweet-Sour Sauce

1 (14-ounce) can pineapple chunks
¾ cup chicken broth or bouillon
2 tablespoons brown sugar
¼ cup vinegar
2 teaspoons soy sauce
1 teaspoon catsup
2 tablespoons cornstarch
½ cup sliced green onions
1 green pepper, cut into 1-inch cubes

Drain pineapple, reserving syrup. In 2½-quart casserole, combine syrup with broth, brown sugar, vinegar, soy, catsup, and cornstarch. Cook by microwave for 4 minutes or until thickened; stir several times. Add pineapple chunks, onions and peppers. Cook 30 seconds longer. Serve with cooked shrimp, pork or chicken.

Butter Crumb Topping

¼ cup butter or margarine
1 cup bread crumbs (soft or dry)
¼ cup shredded cheddar cheese, optional

In 9-inch pie plate, melt butter by microwave for 45 seconds. Stir in bread crumbs and cheese, if desired. Cook by microwave for 1 minute. Sprinkle over cooked broccoli, green beans or stewed tomatoes.

TIPS: Melt butter:
Melt 2 tablespoons butter in 15 seconds; ¼ cup in 30 seconds in glass measuring cup.

Be'chamel Sauce

¼ cup butter or margarine
¼ cup flour
1 cup chicken broth or bouillon
1 cup light cream
½ teaspoon salt
Dash of pepper and paprika

In 4-cup measure, melt butter by microwave. Stir in flour. Cook by microwave for 1 minute, stirring once. Pour in broth, cream, salt, pepper and paprika. Cook by microwave 3 minutes, stirring once every minute. Makes about 2 cups. Serve over chicken, seafood or vegetables.

Basic Creamy Sauce Mix*

1⅓ cups non-fat dried milk powder
¾ cup flour
1 teaspoon salt
½ cup butter or margarine

In mixing bowl, stir together milk powder, flour and salt. With pastry blender, cut in butter until mixture resembles small peas. Refrigerate in tightly covered container. Makes enough sauce for 6 cups medium white sauce.

**To make 1 cup medium white sauce, combine ½ cup basic sauce mix with 1 cup water in 4-cup measure. Cook 4 minutes by microwave, stirring often. Use as sauce for chipped beef, cooked fish or vegetables.*

TIPS: Cream sauces:
Save time by making cream sauces by microwave; stir several times for a smooth product.

Cherry Sauce

¾ cup sugar
2 tablespoons cornstarch
1 (1-pound) can pitted tart red cherries (not drained)
Red food coloring
⅛ teaspoon almond flavoring

In 1½-quart bowl, combine sugar and cornstarch; stir in cherries. Cook by microwave for 6 minutes, stirring often. Stir in several drops food coloring and almond flavoring. Serve over custard, ice cream or angel food cake.

Creamy Scrambled Eggs

6 eggs
¼ cup milk
¼ teaspoon salt
Dash pepper
2 tablespoons butter or margarine
1 (3-ounce) package cream cheese, cut in ½-inch cubes
Chopped chives

Mix eggs with milk, salt and pepper. In 2-quart baking dish, melt butter by microwave. Pour in egg mixture. Cook 3 minutes by microwave, stirring every 30 seconds. Add cheese cubes. Cook 45 to 60 seconds. Sprinkle with chives. Serves 6.

Quiche Lorraine

1 baked 9-inch pie crust
6 slices bacon
½ cup grated Swiss Cheese
3 green onions, thinly sliced
¼ teaspoon salt
¼ teaspoon nutmeg
Dash cayenne pepper
1½ tablespoons flour
2 cups light cream
4 eggs, slightly beaten

Prepare pie crust; cool. Cook bacon by microwave; crumble into small pieces. Sprinkle bacon, cheese and onion over baked crust. In 4-cup measure mix salt, nutmeg, cayenne and flour; gradually stir in milk, blending well. Cook by microwave several minutes or until bubbly; stir every 30 seconds. Slowly stir hot creamy mixture into eggs. Pour over bacon in pie crust. Place shelf in upper position; cook by microwave 3 minutes, 45 seconds; turning once. Brown under infrared browning unit 5 minutes. Let stand 10 minutes.

TIPS: Soften butter and cream cheese:
Soften one stick of butter or 1 (3-ounce) package of cream cheese for 5 seconds in microwave.

Opposite page. Eggs and Cheese; Quiche Lorraine, page 39.

French Toast

2 eggs
¼ teaspoon salt
1 teaspoon sugar
3 tablespoons milk
3 tablespoons butter or margarine
4 slices bread
Cinnamon and sugar

Mix eggs, salt, sugar and milk in shallow bowl. Put butter in 7½ x 12-inch baking dish. Melt butter by microwave. Remove dish from microwave oven. Dip bread into egg mixture. Arrange in hot baking dish with melted butter. Cook by microwave for 1½ minutes. Turn toast over so outer edges are on inside of dish. Cook another 1½ minutes. Sprinkle with cinnamon and sugar. Makes 4 slices toast.

Monterey Fondue

6 slices bread
Soft butter or margarine
1 (8-ounce) can whole kernel corn, drained
2 whole canned green chiles
2 cups shredded Monterey Jack Cheese
3 eggs, slightly beaten
2 cups milk
¾ teaspoon salt

Trim crusts from bread. Spread bread with butter; cut in halves. Arrange half the bread in bottom of 6 x 10-inch baking dish. Cover with half the corn. Seed chiles; cut into strips and arrange half the strips over corn. Sprinkle with half the cheese. Repeat layers. Combine eggs, milk and salt; pour over corn mixture. Cover and refrigerate several hours. Cook, covered, by microwave 6 minutes. Turn dish; uncover and cook another 4 minutes. Makes 5 to 6 servings.

Omelet

4 eggs
4 tablespoons water
Salt and pepper
1 tablespoon butter or margarine
Grated cheese or chopped cooked bacon, optional

Mix eggs with water, salt and pepper. Melt butter in 9-inch pie plate. Pour in egg mixture. Cover with plastic film; cook by microwave 1 minute. Uncover and stir to move cooked edges toward center. Cover and cook an additional 1 minute or 1½ minutes, depending on desired degree of doneness. Let stand 1 minute. If desired, sprinkle with grated cheese or chopped cooked bacon; fold over and heat another 15 seconds. Makes 2 servings.

Eggs Benedict

4 halves toasted English muffins
4 slices cooked ham
4 eggs

Arrange muffin halves in 7½ x 12-inch baking dish. Top with ham. To poach eggs by microwave bring 2 cups water to boil in 1½-quart baking dish. Swirl water with spatula. Drop eggs one at a time, in water; cook until white is firm. Arrange one poached egg on each ham slice. Spoon Hollandaise sauce over all. Cook by microwave about 1 minute or until heated. Makes 4 servings.

Hollandaise Sauce

¼ cup butter or margarine
2 teaspoons lemon juice
2 egg yolks, well beaten
2 tablespoons light cream
⅛ teaspoon salt

In 2-cup glass measuring cup, melt butter by microwave for 30 seconds. Stir in lemon juice, then egg yolks and cream. Cook 15 to 30 seconds or until mixture begins to thicken, stirring once or twice. Remove from heat; beat until smooth.

Meat

The shape of the roast is very important.

A roast will cook more evenly and have a better appearance if the length is greater than the diameter. For a medium or well-done roast select one from the small end of the rib or one that will measure approximately 5 inches in diameter. Uneven roasts cook unevenly. Cover corners or thinner areas with small smooth pieces of foil. Remove foil during last half of cooking in order to cook the portions covered.

There are many factors which influence the number of minutes per pound a cut of meat must be cooked.

1. The temperature of the meat when cooking starts. Start at room temperature if possible. This will reduce cooking time.
2. The doneness desired. Rare meat obviously requires less time.
3. The shape of the meat cut. See above.
4. A boned or rolled roast will cook faster. Bone hinders the penetration of microwaves.
5. Ripened meat cooks faster.
6. Tenderness of the meat cut. The more tender the meat, the faster it will cook.

Use of Metal Rack

Use the metal rack to keep the meat out of the drippings in the bottom of the dish.

Turning over of roast and rotation of cooking dish will give more even cooking.

Place fat side down on the rack for ½ of the cooking time; then place fat side up for the remainder of the cooking time. If more color is needed, turn on infrared browning element and brown as desired.

To determine dish rotation times, multiply the weight of the meat by number of minutes per pound to be cooked. A 5 pound roast to be cooked 7 minutes per pound would be 35 minutes. Divide 35 by 4 equals 8¾ minutes. So at end of 8¾ minutes the dish should be turned front to back. At 17½ minutes the roast should be turned over fat side up; then at 26¼ minutes the dish should be turned front to back for the remaining 8¾ minutes.

Opposite page. Beef; Teriyaki Beef in Bacon, page 49.

Weight of Meat Cut

It is very necessary that you know the exact weight of the meat so you can determine the total cooking time.

Meat Thermometer

Do not use a meat thermometer in the Thermatronic oven as you may damage the thermometer or cause sparking. Remove the food from the oven and then insert the thermometer. Remove the thermometer if you put the food back in the range for further cooking.

Standing Time

After cooking roasts allow 10-15 minutes standing time before carving. A roast will increase 10° to 15° in internal temperature during the standing time.

Cover the roasts with foil to keep the surface hot during standing time. After standing time the temperature should correspond with those given in the following chart for proper doneness.

Meat Roasting Chart

	Temperature after Standing Time	Minutes per Pound
Beef	Rare (140°F)	5-6
	Medium (160°F)	6-7
	Well-Done (170°F)	7-8

Shoulder Clod Roast

4 to 4½ pound shoulder clod roast
Paprika
Pepper
Salt

Sprinkle roast with paprika and pepper. Place fat side up on rack in 7½ x 12-inch baking dish. Cover with plastic wrap. Cook by microwave for 15 minutes. Turn roast. Cover edges of meat with small pieces of foil to prevent over cooking. Cook another 20 minutes. Let stand, covered, for 15 minutes. Sprinkle with salt. Makes 6 to 7 servings. For rare meat, shorten cooking time about 5 minutes; for well-done, add 5 minutes.

Basic Meatballs

3 eggs
½ cup milk
3 cups soft bread crumbs
½ cup finely chopped onion
2 teaspoons salt
3 pounds ground beef

In large mixing bowl, beat eggs. Stir in milk, crumbs, onion and salt. Add meat and mix well. Shape into 72 (1-inch) meat balls. Arrange in large tray; slip tray in plastic bag and tie. Freeze until firm. Repackage in freezer bags, using 24 meat balls per bag. Tie and freeze.

Ground Beef Patties

1 pound ground beef
Salt and pepper

Shape into 4 patties.* Place on rack in 7½ x 12-inch baking dish. Cook by microwave 4 minutes, turning dish once. Sprinkle with salt and pepper.

**For 1 serving, form ¼ pound beef into 1 patty. Cook in small shallow baking dish for 2 minutes, turning dish once.*

Pot Roast In Bag

1 tablespoon flour
1 (10 x 6-inch) plastic cooking bag
2-3 pounds boneless chuck roast (2-inches thick)
1 envelope onion soup mix
½ cup water

Shake flour in empty cooking bag. Place bag in 7½ x 12-inch baking dish. Pour ½ dry soup mix in bag; then slide in meat. Sprinkle top with remaining soup mix; add water. Close bag loosely with rubber band or string about 2-inches from food. Puncture 6 (½″) slits in top of bag with paring knife. Cook 20 minutes by microwave, turning bag once. Let stand 15 minutes. Open bag and serve. Makes 4 to 6 servings.

Individual Meat Loaves

½ cup soft bread crumbs
½ cup evaporated milk
2 eggs, slightly beaten
1 teaspoon salt
⅛ teaspoon pepper
1 small onion, finely chopped
¼ teaspoon ground thyme
1½ pounds lean ground beef
¼ pound process American Cheese

Sauce

¾ cup chili sauce
1 tablespoon Worcestershire sauce
1 teaspoon prepared mustard

In mixing bowl, combine bread crumbs, milk, eggs, salt, pepper, onion and thyme. Add meat; mix well. Cut cheese into 6 cubes. Divide meat into 6 equal portions; form around cheese cubes to make small loaves. Place in 7½ x 12-inch baking dish. Cover with plastic wrap; cook by microwave 4 minutes; turn dish and cook another 4 minutes. Drain fat. Mix chili sauce with Worcestershire and mustard. Pour over meat. Cook, uncovered, for 2 minutes. Makes 6 servings.

Beef Rump Roast

*3½ to 4 pounds beef rump roast, watermelon cut**
Salt and pepper
Seasoned salt

Place roast on rack in 7½ x 12-inch baking dish. Cover with plastic wrap; cook 10 minutes. Cover edges of meat with small pieces of foil to prevent drying. Cover roast; turn baking dish and cook 5 minutes. Turn roast; cover and cook 15 minutes, turning dish once. Let stand, covered for at least 10 minutes before carving. Sprinkle with salt, pepper and seasoned salt. Use drippings for gravy. Makes 5 to 6 servings.

**Watermelon cut is ideal shape for microwave cooking.*

Stuffed Flank Steak

1½ cups packaged bread stuffing
1 (3-ounce) can sliced mushrooms, not drained
2 tablespoons melted butter or margarine
2 tablespoons grated Parmesan cheese
1 flank steak, scored on both sides
2 tablespoons salad oil

Sauce

1 (¾-ounce) package brown gravy mix
¼ cup dry red wine
2 tablespoons minced green onions
¼ cup currant jelly

Combine bread stuffing with mushrooms, butter and cheese. Spread over flank steak; roll up like a jelly-roll. Fasten with wooden skewers or string. Pour oil in 6 x 10-inch baking dish. Roll steak in oil, coating all sides. For sauce; prepare gravy mix according to package directions. Pour gravy, wine and onions over meat. Cover with plastic wrap. Cook by microwave for 20 minutes, turning meat once. Let stand 5 minutes. Remove meat from sauce; add jelly and stir until dissolved. Serve sauce over meat. Makes 4 to 6 servings.

Swiss Steak [in a roasting bag]

1½ pounds round steak
¼ cup flour
1 (1-ounce) package seasoning mix for swiss steak
1 (8-ounce) can tomato sauce
1 cup water

Cut steak into serving-size pieces. Coat with flour. Place in single layer in roasting bag. Combine package of seasoning mix, tomato sauce and water. Pour over steak in bag. Close bag with rubber band or string about 2 inches from end. Place in 7½ x 12-inch baking dish. Puncture 4 holes with fork, in top of bag. Allow to stand 10 minutes. Cook by microwave for 10 minutes. Turn dish and cook another 10 minutes. Let stand 10 minutes. Makes 4 to 5 servings.

Meat Loaf

1½ pounds lean ground beef
1 egg, beaten slightly
½ cup soft bread crumbs
½ cup milk
½ teaspoon salt
¼ cup finely chopped onion
2 tablespoons catsup
1 teaspoon Worcestershire sauce

Combine ingredients; press into 6 x 10-inch loaf shaped baking dish. Cover with plastic wrap. Cook for 10 minutes on lower shelf, turning dish once. Raise shelf. Uncover loaf. Turn on infrared browning unit and brown for 5 minutes. Makes 4 to 6 servings.

Spicy Meatballs

1 tablespoon salad oil
½ clove garlic, minced
24 basic meatballs frozen, (page 45)
1 (8-ounce) can tomato sauce
2 tablespoons dry onion soup mix
1 teaspoon sugar
¾ cup water
½ teaspoon dried oregano, crushed
8 frankfurter buns, split and toasted

In 3-quart shallow casserole, heat oil and garlic. Add meatballs and cook 5 minutes. In 2-cup measure, mix tomato sauce, soup mix, sugar, water, and oregano. Pour over meatballs and cook, covered, 10 minutes. Spoon 3 meatballs with sauce on each frankfurter bun. Makes 8 servings.

TIPS: Thaw ground beef in seven minutes:
If you forget to thaw meat until the last minute, here's a helper. Put 1-pound package of frozen ground beef on folded paper towel in microwave. Turn on microwave for 2 minutes, off for 1 minute; turn on 1 minute, off 1 minute; then on 30 seconds. At this stage, it should be soft enough to unwrap, break apart. To completely thaw, turn off another 1 minute, then on for 30 seconds.

Teriyaki Beef in Bacon

4 slices bacon
1 pound lean ground beef
¼ cup soy sauce
2 tablespoons lemon juice
2 tablespoons honey
1 clove garlic, crushed
¼ teaspoon ground ginger
2 tablespoons white wine

Place bacon on metal rack in 7½ x 12-inch baking dish. Cook by microwave 2 minutes. Form beef into 4 patties; wrap each in slice of bacon. Secure with toothpick. Place in shallow dish. Combine remaining ingredients; pour over meat and refrigerate several hours. Drain; place on metal rack in 7½ x 12-inch baking dish. Cook by microwave 6 to 8 minutes or until desired doneness. Raise shelf and brown with infrared 3 minutes. Makes 4 servings.

Basic Meat Sauce

3 pounds lean ground beef
2 medium onions, chopped
2 cloves garlic, minced
¾ cup finely chopped celery
1 (28-ounce) can tomatoes, cut up
3 (6-ounce) cans tomato paste
2 tablespoons minced parsley
1 teaspoon brown sugar
2 teaspoons salt
1 cup beef bouillon
1 bay leaf
1 tablespoon Worcestershire sauce
½ teaspoon pepper

In 4-quart casserole, combine beef with onions, garlic and celery. Cover with wax paper or plastic wrap; cook by microwave for 10 minutes, stirring twice. Drain excess fat. Add remaining ingredients. Cover and cook 20 minutes, stirring twice. Makes about 3 quarts sauce. Add all or part of sauce to main dishes or freeze for future use. Freeze in 1-quart units, in freezer cartons or jars. Thaw before using in recipes.

Meat and Potato Pie

1 beaten egg
½ cup milk
¾ cup soft bread crumbs
¼ teaspoon salt
Dash pepper
1 pound lean ground beef
⅓ cup chili sauce
½ cup chopped green onion
1 teaspoon prepared mustard
3 cups cooked diced potatoes
½ cup shredded sharp cheddar cheese

Combine egg, milk, crumbs, salt and pepper. Add beef and mix well. Press into bottom and sides of 9-inch pie plate. Cook 2 minutes. Combine chili sauce, onion and mustard. Pour over potatoes; toss lightly. Spoon into baked meat shell. Sprinkle with cheese; cook by microwave 3 minutes. Raise shelf and brown under infrared browning unit 4 minutes. Makes 6 servings.

Cheese-Stuffed Burgers

¾ cup basic creamy sauce mix, (page 36)
1¼ cups milk
1½ cups (6-ounce) shredded sharp process American Cheese
1 slightly beaten egg
1 cup soft bread crumbs
1 pound lean ground beef
1 (3-ounce) can chopped mushrooms, drained
½ cup cooked rice
1 tablespoon chopped green onion

In 1½-quart bowl, combine sauce mix with milk and cheese. Cook by microwave until thick and bubbly, stirring often. In medium mixing bowl, combine egg, ⅓ cup of cooked sauce, and bread crumbs; mix in ground beef. Shape into 4 circles, each 6 inches in diameter. Combine ¼ cup of the mushrooms, all the rice and green onion. Spoon 2 tablespoons mixture into centers. Pull up over edges of stuffing; seal. Cook in 8-inch square baking dish by microwave 7 to 9 minutes. Combine remaining cheese sauce and mushrooms; heat by microwave. Spoon over burgers. Makes 4 servings.

Sweet-Sour Meatballs

24 basic meatballs, (page 45)
1 (8½-ounce) can pineapple tidbits
Water
1 (8-ounce) can whole cranberry sauce
½ cup bottled barbecue sauce
¼ teaspoon salt
Dash pepper
1 tablespoon cornstarch
¼ cup cold water
½ cup chopped green pepper
Hot cooked rice

In 3-quart shallow casserole, cook meatballs for 5 minutes, rearranging several times. Drain excess fat. Drain pineapple, reserving syrup. Add enough water to syrup to make ¾ cup. Combine syrup, cranberry sauce, barbecue sauce, salt and pepper. Pour over meatballs and cook, covered, 10 minutes. Dissolve cornstarch in cold water. Stir into casserole. Cook, stirring often, until mixture thickens. Add pineapple and green pepper. Cook 1 minute. Serve over hot cooked rice. Makes 4 to 6 servings.

Beef-Filled Squash

- 2 medium acorn squash
- 4 slices bacon, diced
- ¼ cup onion, chopped
- ½ teaspoon salt
- 1 pound lean ground beef
- ½ teaspoon salt
- ¼ cup fine dry bread crumbs
- 1 tablespoon melted butter or margarine

Cook whole squash on paper towels by microwave 8 to 10 minutes or until soft. Let stand 5 minutes. In 2-quart shallow casserole, cook bacon and onion for 2 minutes. Add ½ teaspoon salt and meat; cook 5 minutes, stirring often. Cut cooked squash lengthwise; discard seeds and fibers. Carefully remove squash from shells (reserve shells). In small bowl, whip squash with ½ teaspoon salt until squash is fluffy. Combine with beef mixture. Return to squash shells. Top with combination of bread crumbs and butter. Brown with shelf in upper position under infrared browning unit for 4 minutes. Lower shelf and heat by microwave 2 minutes. Makes 4 servings.

TIPS: Meal planning help:

Prepare meat first and let stand to continue cooking while vegetables are cooking.

Opposite page. Pork; Oriental Ham Kabobs, page 54.

Bavarian Pork Chops

1 (1-pound) can sauerkraut, drained
¼ teaspoon caraway seeds
1 cooking apple, cored, peeled and grated
4 loin or rib pork chops
Salt and pepper

In bottom of 7½ x 12-inch baking dish, combine sauerkraut with caraway seeds and apple. Top with chops. Cover with plastic wrap. Cook by microwave for 5 minutes; turn chops and cook another 5 minutes. Sprinkle with salt and pepper. Makes 4 servings.

Oriental Ham Kabobs

1 (17-ounce) can purple plums, pitted and drained
¼ cup orange juice
1 tablespoon chili sauce
1 teaspoon ground ginger
1 teaspoon prepared mustard
1 pound cooked ham, cut into large cubes
½ fresh pineapple, peeled and cut into large cubes or
8 slices canned pineapple, drained and cut into cubes
1 green pepper, cubed
Kumquats, optional

Mash or puree plums; add orange juice, chili sauce, ginger and mustard. Thread ham, pineapple and green pepper on wooden skewers; brush with sauce. Place on rack in 7½ x 12-inch baking dish. Raise shelf to upper position. Preheat infrared browning unit 2 minutes. Brown kabobs under Browning unit for 3 minutes. Turn skewers and brush with sauce. Brown an additional 3 minutes. Lower shelf. Cook kabobs by microwave for 45 seconds. Garnish with kumquats, if desired. Makes 4 servings.

Calico Stuffed Peppers

3 large green peppers
¼ cup water
1 pound bulk sausage
½ cup chopped onion
1 (8-ounce) can whole kernel corn, drained
⅛ teaspoon garlic salt
1 (8-ounce) can tomato sauce
½ cup grated cheddar cheese

Cut peppers in half, lengthwise. Cut stem; scoop out seeds. In covered 4-quart casserole, cook peppers in ¼ cup water for 4 minutes turning dish once. Drain. In 2-quart bowl, cook sausage and onion for 5 minutes, stirring once; drain excess fat. Stir in corn and garlic salt. Place peppers in 7½ x 12-inch baking dish. Spoon meat mixture into peppers. Pour tomato sauce over all. Cover with plastic wrap. Cook by microwave 5 minutes. Sprinkle with cheese and cook, uncovered, an additional 30 seconds. Makes 6 servings.

Pork Chops with Scalloped Potatoes

4 large potatoes, peeled and sliced
1 small onion, sliced
4 pork chops
Salt and pepper
1 (10¾-ounce) can cream of mushroom soup
¾ cup milk

In 7½ x 12-inch baking dish, arrange sliced potatoes and onions. Top with chops; sprinkle with salt and pepper. Combine soup and milk; pour over all. Cover with plastic wrap. Cook by microwave 15 minutes or until potatoes are done, turning dish once. Uncover. Raise shelf; turn on infrared browning unit. Brown for 5 minutes. Makes 4 servings.

Barbecued Spareribs

2½ to 3 pounds spareribs
¼ cup light molasses
⅓ cup chili sauce
1 small onion, minced
1 lemon, thinly sliced
½ teaspoon prepared mustard
1 teaspoon Worcestershire sauce
¼ teaspoon liquid smoke
½ teaspoon celery seed

Cut meat into one or two rib sections. Place on rack in 7½ x 12-inch baking dish. Lightly cover with plastic wrap. Cook by microwave for 6 minutes; turn ribs, cover and cook another 6 minutes. Combine remaining ingredients in 4-cup glass measure. Remove ribs from microwave oven. Cover measuring cup with plastic wrap; cook sauce for 3 minutes. Stir and cook another 2 minutes. Drain fat off ribs. Remove rack and place ribs in bottom of baking dish. Brush heated sauce over ribs. Cover and cook by microwave 5 minutes; turn ribs and brush. Uncover and cook another 6 minutes, brushing and turning once. Makes 4 to 5 servings.

Sausage Patties

1 pound bulk pork sausage

Form sausage into 8 to 10 patties. Lightly cover with paper towel. Cook on rack in 7½ x 12-inch baking dish by microwave 2 minutes. Turn patties; rearrange on rack and cook another minute. For a browner appearance: raise shelf and brown under infrared browning element 4 minutes, rearranging patties once. Makes 4 to 5 servings.

Fresh Pork Sausage Links

Arrange 1 pound sausage links on rack in 7½ x 12-inch baking dish. Cover with paper towel. Cook by microwave 4 to 8 minutes, depending on size of links and degree of doneness; rearrange sausage on rack once. Raise shelf. Brown under infrared browning element 2 or 3 minutes.

Glazed Pork Roast

1 (8-ounce) can crushed pineapple, not drained
1 tablespoon corn syrup
1 cup apricot nectar
2 tablespoons soy sauce
1 tablespoon cornstarch
1 tablespoon lemon juice
3½ to 4 pound pork loin roast
Salt and pepper

In 4-cup measure, combine pineapple, corn syrup, apricot nectar and soy sauce. Dissolve cornstarch in lemon juice; stir into pineapple mixture. Cook by microwave for 4 minutes, stirring once every minute. Set aside. Place roast on rack in 7½ x 12-inch baking dish. Cover with plastic wrap; cook by microwave for 10 minutes, turning dish once. Cover any bones or dry edges with small pieces of foil. Turn roast. Cook, covered, another 10 minutes. Uncover. Sprinkle with salt and pepper. Brush with sauce; cook another 8 minutes. Cover and let stand 10 minutes before carving. Serve with extra sauce. Makes 4 to 6 servings.

Bacon

To cook 4 slices bacon, arrange slices in single layer, on rack in 7½ x 12-inch shallow baking dish. Cover with paper towel (to prevent spattering). Cook by microwave 2¼ to 3 minutes. Rearrange bacon on rack at end of 1½ minutes for more even crispness.

To cook 1 or 2 slices bacon, place on folded paper towels in paper plate, shallow baking dish or regular dinner plate. (Paper towels absorb grease.) Cover with paper towel. Cook 1 slice for 1 to 1½ minutes; 2 slices for 1¼ to 1¾ minutes. Exact cooking time depends on thickness of bacon and fat content.

TIPS: To separate cold bacon:
Heat whole package of cold bacon for 30 seconds by microwave to soften enough to separate individual slices without tearing.

Baked Ham

½ fully cooked ham (5 to 7 pounds) (bone-in shank or butt end)
2 tablespoons honey
¼ cup orange marmalade

Place ham, fat side down, on rack in 7½ x 12-inch shallow baking dish. Cover exposed bone and top edges of ham with small pieces of foil. Loosely cover ham with wax paper. Cook 7 minutes; turn dish and cook another 7 minutes. Turn ham, fat side up, and cook another 10 to 20 minutes*. If glaze is desired, combine honey and marmalade. Remove ham from microwave oven 5 minutes before done. Cut away any rind left on ham; pour off drippings. Score fat; brush with sauce; return to microwave oven. Brush several times during last 5 minutes of cooking. Remove from microwave oven and insert meat thermometer. Temperature should register 115° F. to 120° F. and will increase while standing. Cover ham with foil; let stand 15 to 20 minutes. Serves 10 to 12 people.

**Exact time depends on size of ham and distribution of fat. As a general rule, allow about 7 minutes per pound, total cooking time including standing time for fully cooked bone-in half ham.*

Canned Ham

Place 3 to 5 pound canned ham, fat side down, on rack in 7½ x 12-inch shallow baking dish. Cover with wax paper or plastic wrap. Cook by microwave 5 minutes. Turn dish and cook 5 minutes. Turn ham, fat side up, and cook 5 to 10 minutes. If desired, brush with glaze the last several minutes of cooking. Remove from microwave oven; cover with foil and let stand 10 minutes. Makes 4 to 6 servings.

TIPS: Cooking time:
Be sure to check food at minimum suggested cooking time. Microwave cooking is so fast that a few seconds can dry out food. Exact time varies with original temperature of foods being cooked, as well as size of slices, chunks, etc., of ingredients.

Ham Steak

½ cup brown sugar
1 tablespoon cornstarch
½ teaspoon ginger
1 (12-ounce) can apricot nectar
1 tablespoon lemon juice
1 (1½ to 2-pound) fully cooked ham steak

In 4-cup measure, combine brown sugar with cornstarch. Stir in ginger, apricot nectar and lemon juice. Cook by microwave 4 minutes or until translucent, stirring several times. Set aside. Place ham steak in 7½ x 12-inch shallow baking dish. Cover with plastic wrap or waxed paper. Cook 5 minutes. Turn ham; pour off juices and brush with apricot sauce. Cook another 2 minutes. Makes 4 to 6 servings. Serve with extra sauce.

Marie's Ham with Strawberry Sauce

1 (10-ounce) package frozen strawberries
1 tablespoon cornstarch
Dash cinnamon
Dash ground cloves
1 (3-pound) boneless fully cooked smoked ham

In 1-quart covered casserole, thaw the strawberries 1 minute by microwave. Break up the ice crystals. Add cornstarch, cinnamon and cloves. Stir to a smooth paste. Cook by microwave about 3 minutes or until the sauce is thick and clear. Place the ham on the wire rack in baking dish. Cover with strawberry sauce and cook 4½ minutes. Turn dish around front to back and cook another 4½ minutes. Turn roast over, add more sauce and cook 4½ minutes. Turn dish around front to back and cook another 4½ minutes. Cover with foil and let stand for 10 to 15 minutes before slicing. Warm remaining sauce and serve with ham slices. Serves 4.

TIPS: Meal planning help:
Prepare meat first and let stand to continue cooking while vegetables are cooking.

Teri's Ham Supreme with Holiday Sauce

3-pound fully cooked and boned ham
¾ cup red currant jelly
⅛ teaspoon nutmeg
1 teaspoon grated orange peel
2 tablespoons lemon juice
¼ cup cranberry juice
Whole cloves

Sauce

2 tablespoons cornstarch
½ cup cranberry juice
2 tablespoons orange juice
3 tablespoons lemon juice

In 4-cup measure put currant jelly, nutmeg, orange peel, orange juice, lemon juice and cranberry juice. Bring to a boil for 1½ minutes by microwave. Stir occasionally. Remove syrup from oven and add several drops of red food coloring. Use ⅓ cup of syrup for basting glaze; reserve remainder for Holiday Sauce. Score one surface of ham in diamond design; stud with the whole cloves. Place ham clove side down on rack in baking dish. Allow 6 minutes per pound for cooking the ham (18 minutes). Cook by microwave for 4½ minutes. Baste with glaze. Turn dish around front to back and cook 4½ minutes. Turn ham over, clove side up, baste with glaze and cook 4½ minutes. Baste with glaze and turn dish around front to back and cook 4½ minutes. Brown with infrared browning element for 4 minutes. Remove ham from oven. Cover with foil for the 10 to 15 minute standing time. Serves 4.

Sauce: In a 2-cup measure, mix the cornstarch and cranberry juice until smooth. Blend in the orange and lemon juice and remainder of glaze. Cook by microwave for 2 minutes. Stir and cook 1 minute or until sauce is clear.

TIPS: Meat cooks:
In estimating total meat preparation time, remember to allow 10 or 15 minutes standing time after removal from oven.

Apricot and Prune Stuffed Roast

5-pound pork roast
½ cup diced dried apricots
¼ cup diced dried prunes
2 cups diced cooking apples
2 cups packaged bread stuffing
⅔ cup wine (dry sherry or white)
2 tablespoons butter or margarine

Have the butcher bone and cut a large pocket in the roast for the dressing. In a large bowl combine the apricots, prunes, apples and bread stuffing. In a 2-cup measure heat the butter or margarine with the wine until melted. Pour the butter or margarine and wine over the dressing and toss with fork to combine. Stuff the roast and secure the pocket by sewing it closed with large needle and string. Cook roast fat side down on metal rack in baking dish for 10 minutes. Turn dish front to back and cook another 10 minutes. Turn fat side up and cook 10 minutes. Turn dish front to back and cook another 10 minutes. For that extra golden brown appearance use the infrared browning unit for 5 minutes. Remove roast from the oven and cover with foil for the standing time. Slice and serve. Serves 6 people.

Chicken in the Bag

1 (2½ to 3-pound) frying chicken, cut up
1 (1⅜-ounce) oven cooking bag and sauce mix for chicken
1 (4-ounce) can mushrooms
2 onions, quartered
½ cup catsup

Wash chicken; dry with paper towels. Place chicken in cooking bag, skin side up. Drain mushrooms; save liquid and add water to make ½ cup liquid. Arrange mushrooms and onions around chicken. Blend sauce mix with water, mushroom liquid and catsup. Pour sauce over chicken. Close bag with rubber band or string. Place bag in 7½ x 12-inch baking dish. Punch 4 small holes along top of bag with fork. Cook by microwave for 10 minutes. Turn dish and rearrange chicken; cook another 10 minutes. Let stand 10 minutes. Makes 4 to 5 servings.

Chicken Marengo

2½ pounds frying chicken, cut-up
¼ cup flour
¼ cup oil
1 (1½-ounce) package spaghetti sauce mix
½ cup dry white wine
3 tomatoes, quartered
¼-pound fresh mushrooms

Coat chicken with flour; roll in oil. Place, skin side up, in 7½ x 12-inch baking dish. Cover with plastic wrap and cook by microwave for 8 minutes. Rearrange chicken in dish. Combine spaghetti sauce, wine, and tomatoes. Pour over chicken. Cook 8 minutes. Add mushrooms; cook one minute. Makes 4 to 5 servings.

Opposite page. Poultry; Chicken Marengo, page 63.

Cranberry-Glazed Turkey Roast

1 (3-pound) frozen, boneless, rolled turkey roast
1 (8-ounce) can whole berry cranberry sauce
2 tablespoons orange marmalade
2 tablespoons red wine
¼ teaspoon cinnamon
Melted butter or margarine

Thaw turkey. Heat cranberry sauce, marmalade, wine and cinnamon in 4-cup measure for 2 minutes by microwave; set aside. Cut plastic bag from turkey, but do not remove net. Brush with melted butter. Place turkey on rack in 7½ x 12-inch baking dish. Cover with plastic wrap and cook 15 minutes by microwave, turning dish once. Uncover; turn roast; brush with cranberry mixture. Cook 10 minutes, brushing with sauce and turning roast several times. Cover with plastic wrap and let stand at least 8 minutes. Cut net. Slice turkey. Serve with remaining sauce. Serves 6.

Country Style Chicken

1 frying chicken, cut up
Flour
Pepper
¼ cup butter or margarine
Salt

Coat chicken with flour; sprinkle with pepper. Melt butter in 7½ x 12-inch baking dish by microwave for 2 minutes. Roll chicken in melted butter. Place, skin side up, in baking dish. Cover and cook 4 minutes by microwave. Turn dish; cook 4 minutes. Uncover; rearrange and turn chicken in dish. Cook, uncovered, another 4 minutes. Remove from oven. Raise shelf; preheat infrared browning unit for 1 minute. Brown chicken for 3 minutes. Sprinkle with salt. Makes 4 to 5 servings.

TIPS: Seasoning with salt:
Add salt to water when cooking vegetables or at the end of cooking time for meats. Salt draws moisture from food when cooked in microwave oven.

Roast Chicken

1 roasting chicken (4-4½ pounds)
1 (6½-ounce) package stuffing mix
Salad oil

Rinse chicken; pat dry. Prepare stuffing mix according to package directions. Stuff bird. Tie legs together, tuck wings under. Place, breast side down, on rack in 7½ x 12-inch baking dish. Brush with oil. Cook by microwave 7 minutes. If wings and legs begin to brown too much, cover with small piece of foil. Turn chicken, breast side up; baste with drippings. Cook 7 minutes. Turn dish, cook another 7 minutes. Let stand 10 to 15 minutes before carving. Serves 6.

Stuffed Cornish Hens

¼ cup butter or margarine
¼ cup sliced green onion
¼ cup chopped toasted almonds
2 tablespoons chopped parsley
¼ teaspoon salt
1½ cups cooked rice
4 Cornish game hens
½ cup red wine
½ cup currant jelly
2 tablespoons butter or margarine
2 teaspoons cornstarch
1 tablespoon lemon juice
1 teaspoon Worcestershire sauce

In 4-cup measuring cup, melt ¼ cup butter. Stir in onions, almonds and parsley. Cook by microwave for 2 minutes. Stir in salt and rice. Stuff hens with dressing. Tie legs and wings. Set aside. Combine wine, jelly, 2 tablespoons butter in 2-cup measure. Cook by microwave 1 minute or until jelly melts. Mix cornstarch with lemon juice and Worcestershire. Stir into sauce; cook 1½ minutes, stirring once. Place hens, breast side down, on rack in 7½ x 12-inch baking dish. Brush with sauce. Loosely cover with brown paper. Cook by microwave 12 minutes. Rearrange birds, breast side up, on rack. Brush with sauce and cook another 12 to 14 minutes, brushing with sauce again. Let stand 5 to 10 minutes before serving. Serves 4.

Chicken 'n Rice

2 to 2½ pounds chicken parts
3 tablespoons melted butter or margarine
½ pound brown and serve sausages, cut into chunks
1 (16-ounce) can stewed tomatoes
1 cup chicken bouillon
½ teaspoon salt
1 cup raw regular rice

Place chicken in 3-quart casserole. Pour butter over chicken. Cover and cook by microwave for 8 minutes. Combine remaining ingredients. Spoon over chicken. Cover and cook by microwave another 15 minutes; rearrange chicken parts every 5 minutes. Let stand 10 minutes before serving. Makes 4 to 5 servings.

Hawaiian Fried Chicken

¼ cup soy sauce
¼ cup white wine
Juice of 1 lime
1 clove garlic, minced
¼ teaspoon ground ginger
¼ teaspoon oregano
¼ teaspoon thyme
3 whole chicken breasts, halved
¼ cup flour
½ cup butter or margarine

Combine soy with wine, lime juice, garlic, ginger, oregano and thyme. Pour over chicken; marinate several hours, turning 2 or 3 times. Drain sauce; pat chicken dry with paper towels. Coat with flour. Melt butter in 7½ x 12-inch baking dish. Add chicken, skin side down; spoon butter over chicken. Cook by microwave in upper shelf position for 5 minutes. Turn chicken; brush with butter and cook 6 minutes. Turn on infrared browning unit; cook several minutes or until desired degree of brown. Makes 6 servings.

Chicken Breasts, French Style

3 large chicken breasts, boned, skinned and halved lengthwise
6 slices prosciutto or thinly sliced ham
6 thin slices Swiss or American Cheese
2 tablespoons butter or margarine
Pepper
1 (10¾-ounce) can cream of mushroom soup
2 tablespoons dry white wine
1 (3-ounce) can sliced mushrooms, drained (optional)

Pound chicken breasts with wooden mallet until about ¼-inch thick. Place ham and cheese on each. Tuck in sides and roll up as for jelly roll. Skewer with toothpick or tie securely. Sprinkle with pepper. Cook in butter 3 minutes in 6 x 10-inch baking dish. Turn chicken; cook another 3 minutes. Combine soup with wine and mushrooms. Pour over chicken; cover and cook 7 minutes, turning dish once. Makes 6 servings.

Chicken Dijon

3 tablespoons butter or margarine
4 chicken breasts, split, boned and skinned
2 tablespoons all-purpose flour
1 cup chicken broth
½ cup light cream
2 tablespoons Dijon-style mustard

In 7½ x 12-inch baking dish, melt the butter or margarine by microwave. Using tongs, add the chicken to the butter, coating both sides. Cover and cook by microwave 5 minutes, turn chicken and rearrange so pieces which have been to the inside of the dish are on the outside. Cook 3 minutes longer or until tender. Place on platter. Stir flour into drippings. Add broth and cream. Cook, stirring often, until mixture is thick. Stir in mustard. Return chicken to mixture. Heat 1 minute. Makes 4 servings.

Shake and Bake Chicken

8 chicken parts
1 package seasoned coating mix for chicken

Coat chicken with coating, according to directions on package. Place chicken in 7½ x 12-inch baking dish, skin side down. Cook by microwave for 5 minutes. Turn chicken and cook for 8 minutes. Raise shelf; brown chicken under infrared browning unit for 6 minutes. Makes 4 servings.

Roast Turkey

1 (10-pound) turkey
Salt
2 stalks celery, chopped
1 small onion, chopped
¼ cup butter or margarine
1 (7-ounce) package poultry dressing
¾ cup water
Salad oil

Wash turkey; pat dry with paper towels. Sprinkle inside with salt. In 4-cup measure, combine celery and onion with butter. Cook by microwave for 5 minutes. Add to package dressing with water. Spoon into cavities of turkey. Tie legs together; then to tail. Close neck cavity with small wooden skewer. Tie string around center of turkey to hold wings against body. Place, breast side down, on rack in 7½ x 12-inch shallow baking dish. Brush with salad oil, cover, lightly, with paper bag. Allow about 7 minutes per pound* for total cooking time. Cook ¼ of total time; turn baking dish and brush with drippings. Cook ¼ of time; turn turkey, breast side up, and brush. Cook ¼ of time; turn dish again, brush and cook the final ¼ length of time. Let stand, covered, for 20 minutes. Serves 8.

Poultry Roasting Chart

	Temperature after Standing Time	Minutes per Pound
Poultry	Well-Done 190°	6½-7½

Chicken Ole

6 tortillas, cut into 6 or 8 pieces
2 cups chopped, cooked chicken or turkey
1 (10¾-ounce) can cream of chicken soup
½ cup green chile salsa
½ cup milk
1 teaspoon grated onion
¾ cup grated cheddar cheese

In 1½-quart casserole, arrange alternate layers of tortillas, chicken, and combination of soup with salsa, milk and onion. Sprinkle cheese over top. Refrigerate several hours. Remove from refrigerator. Cover; cook by microwave for 10 minutes or until bubbly. Makes 4 to 5 servings.

Cross-the-road Chicken

1 package frozen green peas with cream sauce
¾ cup milk
1 tablespoon butter or margarine
⅛ teaspoon curry powder
1 cup cooked, diced chicken

Put frozen peas, milk and butter in 1½-quart casserole. Cook covered for 5 minutes by microwave. Remove from oven. Add the curry powder and stir until smooth. Fold in the chicken and cook 1 to 2 minutes or until hot. Serve over rice. 2 or 3 servings.

TIPS: Staggered dinner hours:
If everyone arrives home at a different time, make individual servings on dinner plates; cover and heat each one by microwave when needed.

Deacon's Hot Curried Chicken Bake

1 barbecued chicken
1¼ cups chopped celery
1 small jar chopped pimentos
1 small chopped green pepper
1 small chopped onion
3 chopped hard cooked eggs
1 package coarse chopped cashew nuts
1¼ cups mayonnaise
½ teaspoon salt
⅛ teaspoon pepper
¼ teaspoon celery salt
1/16 teaspoon curry powder
4 tablespoons lemon juice
1 cup chopped cheddar cheese
1½ cups crushed potato chips

Skin and dice the barbecued chicken. In 2-quart flat casserole, mix all the ingredients together with the exception of the cheddar cheese and potato chips. Cook by microwave 3 minutes. Stir and cook 2 minutes. Sprinkle with cheddar cheese and cook 1 minute. Sprinkle with potato chips. Raise shelf to upper position. Place casserole on shelf and brown with infrared browning element 4 to 5 minutes. Serve over rice. Serves 4.

Chicken Cordon Bleu

4 whole chicken breasts (boned) with all the skin possible intact
4 slices Prosciutto or Westphalian ham
4 thin slices Muenster or Monterey Jack cheese
2 tablespoons butter or margarine

Pound each breast until it is thin. Place half slice of ham and cheese on each breast half. Be sure that cheese does not come near the edge of the chicken. Fold the sides together, pinning the edges tightly with round wooden toothpicks (pin through the skin when possible). Melt 2 tablespoons butter or margarine in 7½ x 12-inch baking dish. Coat the chicken in the hot butter or margarine. Place the thick side of the breasts toward the outside of the dish. Cover with plastic wrap and cook 7 minutes by microwave. Turn chicken over, thick side toward the outside of dish. Cover and cook 6 minutes. Preheat the infrared browning element. Remove the plastic wrap. Raise the shelf to the upper position. Brown the chicken with the infrared browning element for 4 minutes. Serve with mushroom sauce. Serves 4.

Mushroom Cheese Sauce

1 tablespoon flour
2 tablespoons grated onion
½ cup grated cheddar cheese
¼ cup milk
1 2½-ounce can mushrooms, sliced and drained
2 tablespoons white wine, optional

Add flour to the fat in dish that Cordon Bleu has been cooked in. Make a smooth paste. Add grated cheese and onion. Mix well. Add milk and wine. Cook until mixture comes to a medium boil. Add mushrooms. Stir often for smoothness. Spoon the hot sauce over the Cordon Bleu.

Mary's Chicken Divan

2 (10-ounce) packages frozen broccoli spears
2 (whole) chicken breasts, boned, skinned and halved
2 cans (10¾-ounce) condensed cream of mushroom soup
1 cup mayonnaise
1 teaspoon lemon juice
½ teaspoon curry powder (optional)
½ cup shredded sharp cheddar cheese
½ cup soft bread crumbs
1 tablespoon butter or margarine

Partially thaw the broccoli in the boxes for 3 minutes by microwave. Place chicken in 7½ x 12-inch baking dish. Cover with plastic wrap and cook 5 to 6 minutes. Remove chicken and slice. Arrange broccoli spears in the baking dish. Place sliced chicken over the broccoli. Combine soup, mayonnaise and lemon juice. Pour over the chicken. Sprinkle with cheese, crumbs and melted butter or margarine. Cover with plastic wrap and cook by microwave 6 minutes. Raise shelf to upper position. Preheat infrared browning element 2 minutes. Remove plastic wrap. Brown 4 minutes with infrared browning element. Makes 4 servings.

TIPS: Cooking time:
Be sure to check food at minimum suggested cooking time. Microwave cooking is so fast that a few seconds can dry out food. Exact time varies with original temperature of foods being cooked, as well as size of slices, chunks, etc., of ingredients.

Opposite page. Seafood; Poached Salmon Steaks, page 75.

Barbecued Halibut Steaks

4 halibut steaks
¼ cup catsup
2 tablespoons salad oil
2 tablespoons lemon juice
1 teaspoon Worcestershire sauce
½ teaspoon prepared mustard
¼ teaspoon garlic salt
Several drops liquid smoke

Arrange halibut steaks on rack in 7½ x 12-inch baking dish. Combine remaining ingredients. Brush fish with sauce. Cook by microwave 3 minutes. Turn fish and brush with sauce. Cook another 3 minutes. Remove from microwave oven. Raise shelf, place baking dish on upper shelf. Turn on infrared browning unit. Brown for 2 minutes. Makes 4 servings.

Shrimp Curry

¼ cup butter or margarine
1 small onion, chopped
¼ cup chopped celery
1 apple, peeled and finely chopped
1 teaspoon salt
1 teaspoon curry powder
¼ cup flour
1 cup chicken broth
1 cup light cream
1 pound cooked and shelled shrimp

In 2½-quart mixing bowl, melt butter by microwave. Add onion, celery and apple; cover and cook 6 minutes or until soft. Stir in salt, curry powder, flour, then broth and cream. Cook another 3 minutes or until thick, stirring once every minute. Add shrimp. Cook 1 minute. Makes 4 to 6 servings.

Poached Salmon Steaks

⅓ cup dry white wine
2 peppercorns
1 bay leaf
1 teaspoon seasoned salt
1 lemon, thinly sliced
1 tablespoon instant minced onion
1½ cups hot water
4 or 5 salmon steaks

Sauce

½ cup dairy sour cream
1 teaspoon lemon juice
1 tablespoon minced parsley
½ teaspoon dried dill weed

In 7½ x 12-inch baking dish, combine wine with peppercorns, bay leaf, seasoned salt, lemon, onion, and water. Heat by microwave for 5 minutes or until boiling. Carefully place fish into hot liquid. Cover and cook 1 minute; turn fish, cover and cook another minute. Let stand 5 minutes. Drain. Combine sauce ingredients; serve with salmon. Makes 4 to 5 servings.

Thermatronic Scampi

1 pound large, raw shrimp
¼ cup butter or margarine
1 clove garlic, minced
2 tablespoons lemon juice
½ teaspoon salt
⅛ teaspoon pepper
1 tablespoon minced parsley

Peel shrimp; split along the back curve, cutting deep, almost to edge; open, then press almost flat, butterfly-style. By microwave, melt butter in 2½-quart baking dish. Pour in garlic and lemon juice. Add shrimp. Stir to coat with butter mixture. Cover and cook 1 minute; uncover, stir and cook another 2 minutes. Sprinkle with salt, pepper and parsley. Makes 3-4 servings.

Fillets Amandine

1 tablespoon butter or margarine
⅓ cup slivered almonds
3 tablespoons butter or margarine
2 tablespoons lemon juice
1½ pounds fish fillets, cut into individual portions
½ teaspoon salt

Combine 1 tablespoon butter and almonds in 9-inch pie plate. Brown on top shelf under infrared browning unit for 5 minutes. Lower shelf. In 7½ x 12-inch baking dish, melt 3 tablespoons butter by microwave; stir in lemon juice. Add fish. Cover and cook by microwave for 2 minutes; turn dish and cook 2 or 3 minutes (depending on thickness of fillets). Sprinkle with salt and toasted almonds. Makes 4 to 5 servings.

Tuna Patties

2 eggs, beaten slightly
1 cup soft bread crumbs
2 teaspoons instant minced onion
1 tablespoon pickle relish
½ teaspoon Worcestershire sauce
2 teaspoons lemon juice
2 (6½-ounce) cans tuna, drained and flaked
2 tablespoons butter or margarine
1 (8-ounce) package peas with cream sauce
2 hard cooked eggs

In bowl, combine eggs with bread crumbs, onion, relish, Worcestershire sauce and lemon juice. Add tuna; mix thoroughly. Shape into 5 or 6 patties (about 2½ to 3 inches in diameter). In 7½ x 12-inch baking dish, melt butter by microwave. Arrange patties in dish with butter. Cover and cook 3 minutes. Turn patties and rearrange in dish. Cover and cook 2 minutes. Raise shelf; brown, uncovered, under infrared browning unit for 5 minutes. To cook peas, combine with amount of milk and butter as indicated on package. Cook in 1½-quart baking dish by microwave for 4 minutes, stirring once. Peel and chop eggs; add to sauce. Spoon over cooked tuna patties. Makes 5 to 6 servings.

Tuna Tetrazzini

2 quarts water
1 teaspoon salt
6 ounces thin spaghetti (about 2 cups)
¼ cup butter or margarine
¼ cup flour
1 cup light cream
1 cup chicken bouillon
2 tablespoons white wine
½ teaspoon seasoned salt
1 (2-ounce) can sliced mushrooms, drained
2 (6½-ounce) cans tuna, drained
½ cup grated cheddar cheese

In 4-quart casserole, heat water and salt to boiling. Break spaghetti into 2-inch pieces; drop in boiling water. Cook for 7 minutes. Let stand while making sauce; then drain. For sauce; melt butter in 2½-quart casserole. Stir in flour, then cream, bouillon, wine and seasoned salt. Cook 1 minute; stir and cook another 2 minutes; stir again and cook 2 minutes. Add mushrooms, tuna and drained spaghetti. Top with cheese. Cook 30 seconds. Makes 5 or 6 servings.

Lobster Tails

2 lobster tails (about 8 ounces each)
¼ cup melted butter or margarine
2 tablespoons lemon juice

Split tails open lengthwise through center of hard top shell and meat, but not through thin under shell. Spread open to expose meat on top. Brush with part of melted butter. Place in shallow baking dish; cover and cook by microwave 2 or 3 minutes or until meat loses its translucency. Pass remaining melted butter and lemon juice. Makes 2 servings.

Seafood Newburg

2 tablespoons butter or margarine
1 cup sliced fresh mushrooms
2 tablespoons flour
1½ cups light cream
2 tablespoons dry white wine
⅛ teaspoon onion salt
½ teaspoon salt
⅛ teaspoon pepper
dash nutmeg
2 egg yolks
1 cup cooked lobster tails, cut into small chunks
1 cup cooked crab meat or shrimp
chopped chives

In 2-quart casserole, melt butter by microwave. Stir in mushrooms, and flour; then cream, wine and seasonings. Cook by microwave 4 minutes, stirring often. Beat egg yolks; stir part of sauce into yolk. Then return to casserole. Cook another minute, stirring every 15 seconds. Stir in seafood and cook 30 seconds or until hot. Sprinkle with chives. Serve over baked patty shells or toast cups. Makes 4 to 5 servings.

Sole Veronique

1 pound fillet of sole
1 cup sauterne wine
¼ cup butter or margarine
1 tablespoon cornstarch
⅔ cup light cream
½ teaspoon salt
1 cup seedless grapes

Cut fish into serving size portions. In 7½ x 12-inch baking dish, pour ⅔ cup wine over fish. Reserve ⅓ cup. Cover with plastic wrap and cook by microwave 4 minutes, turning dish once. Drain fillets. In 4-cup measure, melt butter by microwave. Dissolve cornstarch in cream; stir into melted butter. Add ⅓ cup reserved wine to cream mixture. Cook by microwave 2½ minutes, stirring every 30 seconds. Add grapes. Place cooked sole in heat proof platter. Pour sauce with grapes over fish. Cook by microwave 30 seconds. Makes 3 to 4 servings.

Salmon Newburg

½ cup basic creamy sauce mix, (page 36)
1 cup light cream
½ cup water
3 slightly beaten egg yolks
3 tablespoons dry white wine
2 teaspoons lemon juice
¼ teaspoon salt
¼ teaspoon dried tarragon, crushed
1 (16-ounce) can salmon, drained, broken into chunks, and bones removed
4 frozen patty shells, baked

In 2-quart casserole, combine sauce mix, cream and water. Cook by microwave until thickened and bubbly, stirring often. Stir small amount of hot mixture into egg yolks. Return mixture to casserole; cook, stirring often, about 1 minute or until thick. Stir in wine, lemon juice, salt and tarragon. Add salmon chunks and cook by microwave until hot. Spoon over baked patty shells. Makes 4 servings.

Knockwurst and Hot German Potato Salad

3 medium potatoes
3 slices bacon, diced
1 small onion, diced
1 tablespoon flour
1 tablespoon sugar
1 teaspoon dry mustard
1 teaspoon salt
¼ teaspoon pepper
¼ cup vinegar
½ cup water
½ teaspoon celery seeds
4 knockwurst
1 tablespoon finely chopped parsley

Wash potatoes; dry and cut into half. Place in plastic bag, cut side down. Leave end of bag open. Cook by microwave for 10 minutes or until tender. Remove skins and slice. Cook bacon and onion in 4-cup measure for 4 minutes. Stir in flour, sugar, mustard, salt and pepper; mix well. Add vinegar, water and celery seeds. Cook another 4 minutes, stirring once. Set aside. Make several cuts in plastic bag holding knockwurst. Place on paper plate. Cook by microwave 1½ minutes. Cut each knockwurst into 6 pieces. Arrange meat and cooked potatoes in shallow bowl. Pour hot sauce over; toss to coat evenly. Sprinkle with chopped parsley. Serve immediately. Makes 4 servings.

Chili Dog Casserole

1 (15-ounce) can chili with beans
1 (12-ounce) can whole kernel corn, drained
6 frankfurters
6 strips cheddar cheese (about ½-inch x 3-inches)
1 (8-ounce) can tomato sauce
1 tablespoon chopped green onion

Combine chili with corn in 6 x 10-inch baking dish. Split franks down middle, being careful not to cut through. Insert 1 strip cheese in each frankfurter. Place on top of beans, spoon tomato sauce and onion over all. Cover and cook by microwave for 9 minutes; turn dish and cook another 2 minutes. Makes 4 to 6 servings.

Opposite page. Other meats; Knockwurst and Hot German Potato Salad, page 81.

Minted Lamb Chops

½ cup wine vinegar
½ cup apple-mint jelly
2 tablespoons brown sugar
1 tablespoon lemon juice
1 teaspoon grated lemon peel
½ teaspoon dry mustard
6 loin lamb chops
Salt and pepper

In 4-cup measure, combine vinegar, jelly, sugar, lemon juice, lemon peel and mustard. Heat by microwave for 2 minutes or until jelly melts. Cool slightly; pour over lamb chops. Marinate several hours. Drain, reserving marinade. Place lamb chops on rack in 7½ x 12-inch baking dish. Brush with sauce. Cover loosely with plastic wrap. Cook by microwave for 5 minutes; turn chops and brush with sauce. Cook another 5 minutes. Sprinkle with salt and pepper. Makes 3 servings.

Veal Scaloppine

1 pound thin veal cutlets
¼ cup flour
¼ cup butter or margarine
1 clove garlic, minced
4 large mushrooms, sliced
¼ cup dry white wine
1 chicken bouillon cube
¼ cup hot water
Salt and pepper

Cut veal into serving size pieces; coat with flour. In 7½ x 12-inch baking dish, melt butter with garlic by microwave. Stir in meat. Cook 2 minutes; turn dish and cook another 2 minutes. Add mushrooms, wine, bouillon dissolved in hot water. Cover with plastic wrap. Cook by microwave for 2 minutes. Add salt and pepper. Makes 4 servings.

Meat Roasting Chart

	Temperature after Standing Time	Minutes per Pound
Lamb	Well-Done 180°	7½-8½

Veal Chop Suey

3 tablespoons butter or margarine
2 cups thinly sliced veal
2 tablespoons flour
1½ cup diced celery
1 cup chopped onions
1 teaspoon salt
⅛ teaspoon pepper
1 cup chicken bouillon
1 cup bean sprouts
½ cup canned mushroom pieces
1 tablespoon soy sauce
1 tablespoon Worcestershire sauce
1 tablespoon cornstarch
¼ cup cold water

Melt butter in 2-quart bowl by microwave. Dip veal in flour; add to butter. Cook 5 minutes, stirring once. Stir in celery, onions, salt, pepper, and bouillon. Cook 10 minutes by microwave. Add bean sprouts, mushrooms, soy and Worcestershire. Cook 2 minutes. Dissolve cornstarch in cold water; stir into meat mixture. Cook 1 minute. Serve with rice or noodles. Makes 4 to 6 servings.

Lemon-Butter Glazed Lamb Roast

1 (5-pound) lamb roast, boned
Freshly ground pepper
1 teaspoon ground oregano
3 garlic cloves
¼ cup butter
⅓ cup lemon juice
1 teaspoon soy sauce

Sprinkle all sides of lamb with pepper and oregano. Cut one garlic clove and rub over roast. Crush remaining garlic. Melt butter in 1-cup glass measure; add lemon juice, soy and remaining garlic. Heat 1 minute by microwave. Place roast, skin side down, on metal rack in 7½ x 12-inch baking dish. Pour ½ glaze over meat; cook by microwave for 20 minutes. Turn roast over; pour remaining glaze over meat and cook by microwave for additional 15 minutes. Protect edges from overcooking with small pieces of foil. Remove from oven; cover with foil and let stand 20 minutes. Makes about 6 servings.

Heating of Precooked Frozen Casseroles

Many of the beef and one-dish recipes given can be frozen and heated later.

If you are freezing casserole dishes:

1. Freeze in microwave oven-proof dishes that have tight fitting covers. If this is not possible, wrap with foil for freezing. Then remove foil and cover dish with plastic wrap for heating.
2. Place the food in 2 casseroles not in one large one, for more even defrosting and heating.
3. Turn dishes. Casseroles may be more evenly heated by giving dish ¼ to ½ turn once or twice during the heating time.

If casserole cannot be stirred (Lasagna for example) cut crosswise through the center of the mixture before freezing. Using the cutting knife, spread this cut open as far as possible to expose as much center mixture as possible to the microwave when heating.

Cooking times of the frozen casserole will be about twice as long as the unfrozen food. After ½ of the cooking time when you turn the dish, let the food rest for 5 minutes while conduction heat goes to the center.

Tacos

1 pound lean ground beef
1 (1¼-ounce) package taco seasoning mix
1 cup hot water
6-7 cooked taco shells
2 cups shredded lettuce
2 medium tomatoes, chopped
Grated cheese

In 2-quart casserole, crumble beef; cook for 4 minutes, stirring once. Drain fat; stir in seasoning mix and water. Cover lightly with paper towel; cook for 5 minutes, stirring once. Heat cooked taco shells on paper towel or paper plate by microwave for 30 seconds. Fill shells with ground beef mixture, lettuce, tomatoes and cheese. Makes 6 or 7 tacos.

Preceding page. One-Dish Meals, clockwise from top; Tacos, page 86; Hacienda Holiday Casserole, page 94; Corned Beef and Cabbage, page 96; Fiesta Bake, page 96; Oriental Supper, page 98.

Polish Noodles

8 ounces noodles
1 pound ground beef
2 (8-ounce) cans tomato sauce
Salt and pepper
¼ cup chopped green onions
2 tablespoons chopped green pepper
1 cup dairy sour cream
1 (8-ounce) carton cottage cheese
1 (8-ounce) package cream cheese

In 4-quart casserole, cook noodles in 2½ quarts boiling water until tender; drain. Cook beef by microwave about 4 minutes, stirring once to break up chunks of meat; drain excess fat. Add tomato sauce, salt and pepper; cook 5 minutes by microwave. Combine onions, green pepper, sour cream and cheeses. In casserole, layer half the noodles, all the cheese mixture, the remaining noodles; then all the meat sauce. Cover with plastic wrap; cook by microwave 15 minutes. Makes 6 servings.

Mandarin Style Steak

1½ pounds round steak (about ½-inch thick)
2 tablespoons salad oil
1 (1⅜-ounce) envelope onion soup mix
2 tablespoons soy sauce
¼ teaspoon ground ginger
1 cup water
1 (8½-ounce) can water chestnuts, drained and sliced
½ green pepper, sliced
1 tomato, cut into wedges
2 tablespoons toasted sesame seeds

Cut steak into ¼-inch wide strips. In 3-quart casserole, heat oil 2 minutes by microwave. Add meat; cook 3 minutes; rearrange and cook 1½ minutes. Stir in soup mix, soy, ginger and water. Cover and cook 7 minutes or until tender. Stir in water chestnuts, green pepper and tomato. Cook 1 minute. Sprinkle with sesame seeds. Serve with crisp Chinese noodles. Makes 4 to 5 servings.

Chile Steaks

2 tablespoons flour
1 teaspoon chili powder
1½ pounds round steak, cut into 4 or 5 pieces
2 tablespoons salad oil
1 onion, sliced
1 (8-ounce) can tomatoes
1 (15-ounce) can chili with beans
1 teaspoon salt
½ cup grated cheddar cheese

Combine flour and chili powder in plastic or paper bag. Pound meat with meat mallet or edge of saucer. Add to flour in bag; shake until coated. Pour oil into 7½ x 12-inch baking dish; heat by microwave for 2 minutes. Add meat; turn to coat both sides with hot oil. Cook 4 minutes. Turn and rearrange meat in dish. Add onion and cook 4 minutes. Combine tomatoes, beans and salt. Pour over meat. Cover with plastic wrap; cook by microwave 15 minutes, turning dish at least once. Uncover; sprinkle with cheese. Cook another 30 seconds. Makes 4 to 5 servings.

Beef Enchiladas with Cheese

1 pound lean ground beef
1 cup grated Monterey Jack or cheddar cheese
1 (2½-ounce) can sliced ripe olives, drained
1 (6-ounce) can tomato paste
1 (1⅝-ounce) package enchilada sauce mix
3 cups warm water
8 corn tortillas
1½ cups grated Monterey Jack or cheddar cheese

In 1½-quart casserole, crumble meat. Cook by microwave 4 minutes, stirring twice. Drain fat. Add 1 cup cheese and olives to meat. In 2½-quart casserole, blend tomato paste with enchilada sauce mix; stir in water. Cover and cook by microwave for 8 minutes. Pour 1 cup prepared enchilada sauce in 7½ x 12-inch baking dish. Dip each tortilla into remaining heated sauce. Spoon beef mixture in center of each tortilla. Fold sides of tortilla over filling and place in baking dish, seam side down. Pour remaining sauce over. Top with 1½ cups cheese, cover with plastic wrap. Heat by microwave for 2 minutes. Turn baking dish and cook another minute. Makes 8 enchiladas.

New England Meat Pie

1 pound lean ground beef
1 egg, beaten slightly
¼ cup fine dry bread crumbs
2 tablespoons milk
1 teaspoon salt
1 (10-ounce) package frozen mixed vegetables, partially thawed
¼ teaspoon thyme
¼ teaspoon pepper
1 (8-ounce) can tomato sauce
1 (12-ounce) package frozen hash brown potatoes, thawed
2 tablespoons salad oil
¼ cup grated cheese

Combine beef with egg, bread crumbs, milk and salt. Shape into 1-inch balls. Place on rack in 7½ x 12-inch baking dish; cover and cook by microwave for 5 minutes. Drain. Combine with vegetables, thyme, pepper and tomato sauce. Press potatoes on bottom and sides of regular 10-inch pie pan or 9-inch deep dish pie pan; drizzle with oil. Place on top shelf under infrared browning unit for 5 minutes. Spoon meat ball mixture over potatoes. Lower shelf and cook 5 minutes by microwave. Sprinkle with cheese and heat 15 seconds. Makes 5 servings.

Chili Con Carne

1 pound ground beef
1 cup chopped onion
½ cup chopped green pepper
1 (16-ounce) can tomatoes, cut up
2 (16-ounce) cans dark red kidney beans, drained
1 (8-ounce) can tomato sauce
1 teaspoon salt
¼ teaspoon garlic powder
1 to 2 teaspoons chili powder

In 3-quart casserole, cook meat, onion, and green pepper by microwave for 5 minutes or until vegetables are tender, stirring once. Stir in remaining ingredients. Cover; cook by microwave for 15 minutes, stirring once. Makes 6 servings.

Ruth's Shell Casserole

6 ounces large shell-shaped macaroni
1 pound lean ground beef
1 small onion, chopped
1 teaspoon salt
¼ teaspoon garlic powder
1 teaspoon Worcestershire sauce
¼ cup flour
1 (10½-ounce) can beef bouillon soup
1 (2-ounce) can sliced mushrooms, drained
2 tablespoons red wine
1 cup dairy sour cream
finely chopped parsley

In 4-quart casserole, bring 2 quarts water to boil by microwave. Drop in macaroni. Cook 8 minutes; let stand while preparing sauce. In 3-quart casserole, break up beef with fork; add onion and cook by microwave 4 minutes. Stir in salt, garlic powder, Worcestershire and flour; mix well. Add soup and mushrooms. Drain cooked macaroni; stir into meat mixture. Cover and cook by microwave 5 minutes, stirring once. Add wine and sour cream. Heat 30 seconds. Sprinkle with parsley. Makes 4 to 5 servings.

Spaghetti

8 cups water
1 teaspoon salt
8 ounces spaghetti

In 4-quart casserole, heat water and salt to boiling by microwave. Stir in spaghetti and cook, uncovered, for 7 to 9 minutes or until firm but tender. Cover and let stand 5 minutes. Drain. Makes 4 servings.

TIPS: Heat tortillas:
Place package of tortillas in microwave; cook 2 minutes; pause 15 seconds. Turn package a half turn and cook an additional 2 minutes or until heated through.

Spaghetti with Meat Sauce

1 pound lean ground beef
1 medium onion, chopped
1 clove garlic, minced
1 (28-ounce) can tomatoes, cut-up
½ cup chopped celery
¼ cup burgundy wine
1 cup water
1 (6-ounce) can tomato paste
2 tablespoons chopped parsley
1 tablespoon brown sugar
1 teaspoon dried oregano leaves, crushed
1 teaspoon salt
¼ teaspoon dried thyme leaves, crushed
1 bay leaf
8 ounces spaghetti
Parmesan cheese

In 4-quart casserole, crumble meat; add onion. Cook for 4 minutes, stirring twice. Add remaining ingredients except spaghetti and cheese. Cover and cook 5 minutes. Stir; cover and continue cooking 10 minutes, stirring at least once. Cook spaghetti; drain. Spoon sauce over spaghetti; sprinkle with cheese. Makes 4 to 5 servings.

Spoonburgers

1½ pounds lean ground beef
1 medium onion, chopped
1 (10½-ounce) can condensed tomato soup
1 tablespoon vinegar
2 tablespoons water
1 tablespoon brown sugar
1 teaspoon chili powder
1 teaspoon Worcestershire sauce
¼ teaspoon celery salt
½ teaspoon salt
5 to 6 hamburger buns

In 3-quart casserole, cook beef and onion by microwave for 6 minutes, stirring several times to break up chunks of meat, or until onion is soft. Combine remaining ingredients except buns and pour over meat. Cook 8 minutes. Spoon over warm hamburger buns. Makes 5 to 6 servings.

Pizza Burgers

2 pounds lean ground beef
½ cup grated mozzarella cheese
2 tablespoons grated parmesan cheese
1 teaspoon instant minced onion
½ teaspoon salt
¼ cup chopped ripe olives
1 (8-ounce) can tomato sauce
½ teaspoon oregano
½ teaspoon garlic salt

Divide meat into 4 large patties about 6 inches in diameter. Combine mozzarella, parmesan, onion, salt, and olives. Place one quarter of cheese mixture in center of each burger. Fold over, press edges together. Place on rack in 7½ x 12-inch baking dish. Cover with plastic wrap and cook in microwave oven 4 minutes. Turn dish; cook 2 minutes. Rearrange meat on rack. Cook 2 to 4 minutes, depending on desired doneness. Combine tomato sauce with oregano and garlic salt in 2-cup measure. Heat by microwave for 1 minute. Serve with burgers. Makes 4 generous servings.

Beef Stroganoff

¼ cup butter or margarine
1½ pounds beef sirloin, cut in ½ x 2-inch strips
¼ cup flour
1 small onion, chopped
¼ pound fresh mushrooms, sliced
1 beef bouillon cube
¾ cup boiling water
2 tablespoons tomato paste
1 teaspoon Worcestershire sauce
¾ teaspoon salt
1 cup dairy sour cream

In 3-quart casserole, melt butter by microwave. Coat beef with flour. Add to butter in casserole. Cook, uncovered, for 3 minutes; turn meat and cook another 2 minutes. Stir in onions and mushrooms. Cook 2 minutes, stirring once. Dissolve bouillon in boiling water. Pour bouillon, tomato paste, Worcestershire, and salt into casserole with meat. Cover and cook 5 minutes. Let stand 2 minutes. Uncover; stir in sour cream. Makes 4 to 5 servings.

Lasagne International

1 pound Italian sausage, casings removed
1 (16-ounce) can tomatoes, cut up
1 (6-ounce) can tomato paste
¼ teaspoon dried basil, crushed
⅛ teaspoon garlic salt
16 ounces Ricotta or cottage cheese
¼ cup grated Parmesan Cheese
1 tablespoon chopped parsley
1 egg, beaten slightly
½ teaspoon salt
⅛ teaspoon pepper
8 ounces lasagna noodles
8 ounces Mozzarella Cheese, sliced

In 3-quart casserole, break up sausage and cook by microwave 3 minutes, stirring once. Drain excess fat. Add tomatoes, tomato paste, basil and garlic salt. Cook, uncovered, by microwave 10 minutes, stirring twice. In mixing bowl, stir together Ricotta, Parmesan, parsley, egg, salt and pepper. Bring to boil 2½ quarts water in 4-quart casserole; drop in lasagna noodles and cook 10 minutes. Drain. Spoon a little sauce in bottom of 7½ x 12-inch baking dish. Arrange half the cooked noodles over sauce; then half the Ricotta mixture, half the Mozzarella and half the meat sauce. Repeat. With sharp knife, cut crosswise through mixture at center of dish to allow microwaves to penetrate more quickly. Cook by microwave 3 minutes. Turn dish and cook 4 minutes. Let stand 10 minutes. Makes 6 to 7 servings.

TIPS: Cooking time:
Be sure to check food at minimum suggested cooking time. Microwave cooking is so fast that a few seconds can dry out food. Exact time varies with original temperature of foods being cooked, as well as size of slices, chunks, etc., of ingredients.

Swedish Cabbage Rolls

1 egg
1 teaspoon Worcestershire sauce
¼ cup onion, chopped fine
⅔ cup milk
1 pound lean ground beef
¾ cup cooked rice
6 large leaves cabbage
1 (10½-ounce) can condensed tomato soup
1 tablespoon brown sugar
1 tablespoon lemon juice

In bowl, combine egg, Worcestershire, onion and milk; mix well. Add beef and rice; beat together with fork. Place cabbage leaves in 4-quart deep casserole with 2 tablespoons water. Cover and cook by microwave 8 minutes. Let stand, covered, until cool. Split thick part of leaf about 2 inches. Spoon ½ cup meat mixture on each leaf. Fold in sides and roll ends over meat. Secure with toothpicks. Place rolls in 7½ x 12-inch baking dish. Combine soup, sugar and lemon juice. Pour over cabbage. Cover with plastic wrap. Cook 10 minutes. Makes 6 servings.

Hacienda Holiday Casserole

1 quart basic meat sauce
2 tablespoons chopped canned green chiles
1 cup refried beans
6 corn tortillas, cut in eighths
1 (2¼-ounce) can sliced ripe olives, drained
2 cups grated cheddar cheese

In 2-quart casserole, combine meat sauce with chiles and refried beans. Arrange alternate layers of sauce with tortillas, olives and cheese. Cook by microwave for 7 minutes, turning casserole twice. Makes 5 to 6 servings.

Beef Noodle Pie

2 cups uncooked green noodles
¼ cup butter or margarine
¼ cup Parmesan Cheese
2 tablespoons salad oil
¾ cup chopped onion
2 cloves garlic, crushed
1½ pounds lean ground beef
½ cup water
2 tablespoons sherry wine
1 tablespoon Worcestershire sauce
2 beef bouillon cubes
1 teaspoon salt
¼ teaspoon pepper
2 cups grated Gouda or cheddar cheese
¼ cup grated Parmesan Cheese

Bring 6 cups hot water to boil in 4-quart bowl. Add noodles and cook, uncovered, 7 minutes. Stir twice. Cover and let stand 10 minutes. Drain well. Add butter and ¼ cup Parmesan Cheese; toss well. Place on bottom and sides of 10-inch pie plate. Set aside. Combine oil with onion and garlic in 3-quart casserole. Cook 3 minutes. Stir in beef; cook until it loses red color. Add water, sherry, Worcestershire, bouillon cubes, salt and pepper; cook 3 minutes. Stir 1½ cups Gouda Cheese into meat mixture. Pour into noodle-lined pie plate. Sprinkle with remaining Gouda and ¼ cup Parmesan Cheese. Cook by microwave until bubbly hot. Makes 6 servings.

TIPS: Thaw ground beef in seven minutes:

If you forget to thaw meat until the last minute, here's a helper. Put 1-pound package of frozen ground beef on folded paper towel in microwave. Turn on microwave for 2 minutes, off for 1 minute; turn on 1 minute, off 1 minute; then on 30 seconds. At this stage, it should be soft enough to unwrap, break apart. To completely thaw, turn off another 1 minute, then on for 30 seconds.

Fiesta Bake

1 quart basic meat sauce
1 teaspoon chili powder
1 (12-ounce) can whole kernel corn, not drained
1 (8½-ounce) package corn muffin mix
1 teaspoon sugar
1 egg
⅓ cup milk
Chopped chives

Mix meat sauce with chili powder and corn. Spoon into 7½ x 12-inch baking dish. Cover with wax paper or plastic wrap. Cook by microwave 3 minutes; uncover. In the meantime, combine muffin mix with sugar, egg and milk. Drop by tablespoon on top of hot meat mixture. Sprinkle with chives. Cook by microwave for 5 minutes, turning dish once. Raise shelf, brown under infrared browning unit 3 minutes, turning dish several times. Makes 6 servings.

Corned Beef and Cabbage

3½ to 4 pound round of corned beef
Water
3 medium potatoes, peeled and quartered
3 carrots, quartered
1 small head cabbage, cut into wedges

In 4-quart casserole, cover corned beef with water. (Add packet of seasonings, if bought with meat.) Cook, covered 30 minutes. Turn meat over and cook another 30 minutes. Add potatoes and carrots; cook covered for 20 minutes. Add cabbage and cook 10 minutes or until vegetables are tender. Let stand, covered, for 10 minutes. To serve, remove corned beef and vegetables to platter, using slotted spoon. Makes 6 servings.

TIPS: Rotate position of baking dishes:
For quick and even cooking, remember to rotate dishes at least once while cooking by microwave.

Country Garden Bake

2 pounds lean ground beef
1 clove garlic, crushed
1 cup chopped onion
1 (3-ounce) can sliced mushrooms
Salt and pepper
1 (10-ounce) package frozen Mexican corn with butter sauce
1 (10-ounce) package frozen peas in butter sauce
Instant mashed potatoes (serving for 4)
¼ cup grated cheddar cheese
2 tablespoons butter or margarine
4 tablespoons grated Romano Cheese

In 2-quart bowl, break up meat with fork. Cook by microwave 5 to 6 minutes or until meat loses its red color; stir often. Drain excess fat. Add garlic, onion, and mushrooms; cook 3 minutes. Sprinkle with salt and pepper. Thaw corn in covered 1½-quart bowl for 2 minutes; stir, cook 1 minute. Repeat with peas. In 2-quart casserole, place half the meat mixture, then corn; the other half of meat, then peas. Cook covered 6 minutes. Prepare instant potatoes according to package directions for serving of 4. Spoon over peas. Sprinkle cheddar cheese on top. Dot with butter. Raise shelf to upper position; brown under infrared browning unit 3 minutes. Sprinkle with Romano Cheese. Brown 4 to 6 minutes. Makes 6 to 8 servings.

Mock Lasagne

1 quart basic meat sauce, (page 50)
½ teaspoon dried oregano leaves, crushed
¼ teaspoon dried thyme leaves, crushed
¼ pound Monterey Jack Cheese, thinly sliced
1 cup cottage cheese
6 ounces medium noodles, cooked and drained
¼ cup grated Parmesan Cheese

Combine meat sauce with oregano and thyme. Spread ⅓ the meat sauce in bottom of 7½ x 12-inch baking dish; half the Jack Cheese, half the cottage cheese and half the noodles. Repeat, using ⅓ more of the meat sauce and remaining Jack Cheese, cottage cheese and noodles. Spread with remaining meat sauce. Sprinkle with Parmesan Cheese. Cover with waxed paper. Cook by microwave for 4 minutes; turn dish and cook another 4 minutes. Let stand several minutes before serving. Makes 6 servings.

Oriental Supper

24 basic meatballs, (page 45)
1 (10½-ounce) can condensed beef broth
1 soup can water
1 medium onion, sliced
1½ cups bias-sliced celery (½-inch pieces)
1 (16-ounce) can chop suey vegetables, drained
1 (6-ounce) can mushrooms
3 tablespoons cornstarch
½ cup cold water
3 tablespoons soy sauce
1 (3-ounce) can chow mein noodles

In 3-quart shallow casserole, cook meatballs by microwave for 5 minutes, rearranging meat several times. Add beef broth and soup can of water. Stir in onion and celery. Cook, covered for 10 minutes. Add chop suey vegetables and mushrooms. Blend cornstarch with ½ cup cold water and soy sauce. Add to casserole. Cook, covered, 5 minutes or until mixture thickens, stirring several times. Serve over noodles. Makes 5 to 6 servings.

Meatball Garden Dish

24 basic meatballs, (page 45)
1 (10½-ounce) can condensed beef broth
1 soup can water
3 medium potatoes, peeled and quartered
6 medium carrots, peeled, quartered and halved
1 medium onion, sliced
1 (10-ounce) package frozen peas
2 tablespoons water
⅓ cup flour
⅔ cup cold water

In 3-quart shallow casserole, cook meatballs 5 minutes by microwave, rearranging meat several times. Pour in broth and soup can of water. Add potatoes, carrots and onion. Cover and cook in microwave 15 to 20 minutes or until vegetables are tender. Combine peas and 2 tablespoons water in 1-quart casserole. Cook, covered, 5 minutes. Add to meatball mixture. With slotted spoon, remove meat and vegetables to serving dish. Combine flour with ⅔ cup water. Stir into drippings in 3-quart casserole. Cook by microwave 5 minutes or until thick, stirring several times. Pour part of gravy over vegetables and meat; pass remaining gravy. Makes 6 servings.

Confetti Meatball Supper

1 (10-ounce) package frozen mixed vegetables
2 teaspoons water
3 cups cooked rice
2 tablespoons melted butter or margarine
24 basic meatballs, (page 45)
½ cup finely chopped onion
1 (10¾-ounce) can condensed cream of mushroom soup
1 (11-ounce) can condensed cheddar cheese soup
½ cup catsup
2 tablespoons Worcestershire sauce

Cook mixed vegetables and water in covered 1-quart casserole for 6 minutes; drain and mix with cooked rice and butter or margarine. Press lightly into greased 5½-cup ring mold. In shallow 3-quart casserole cook meatballs and onion for 5 minutes; drain excess fat. Mix soups, catsup and Worcestershire; pour over meatballs. Cook, covered, 10 minutes. Unmold rice ring on ceramic serving platter. Cover with wax paper and heat by microwave 4 minutes. Fill center of ring with meatballs and some of the sauce. Pass remaining sauce. Makes 4 to 6 servings.

Au Gratin
POTATOES
Tender potato slices with a special tangy Cheddar cheese sauce mix.
MAKES 6 (1/2 CUP) SERVINGS
NET WT 5.5 OZ
Macaroni & Cheese
DELUXE DINNER
Complete with ready-made sauce!

Convenience Food Guide

TV dinners and casseroles frozen in foil containers may be heated in your Thermatronic oven as long as the depth of the container is no more than ⅞". If deeper containers are used the food will be shielded by the metal and will not heat through.

Open the package of the frozen TV meal, remove the foil lid and remove the bread and the soup. If left in the container the bread could be overcooked and dehydrated by the time the rest of the food is serving temperature. The soup is easily spilled. Heat bread and soup separately.

Put the tray back into the original package, close loosely and heat according to the instructions on the chart.

If your microwave oven is not a Thermador, follow the manufacturer's instruction for the use of metal.

Instant Potatoes (for 4)

In 4-cup measure put 1⅓ cups water, ⅓ cup milk, ½ teaspoon salt and 2 tablespoons butter or margarine, bring just to boiling 4 minutes.

Remove from oven, stir in 1⅓ cups instant potatoes and whip with fork to consistency desired.

If making 8-12 servings follow same procedure, using a larger, deep bowl for bringing water, milk and butter or margarine to a boil.

Skillet and Casserole Mixes

In 3-quart shallow casserole, brown the ground beef by microwave for 4 minutes. Stirring often so meat will be crumbly. Add the remaining ingredients and water. Cover and cook 8 minutes, stirring after 4 minutes and 6 minutes of cooking time. Leave covered at end of cooking time for 5 minutes of standing time.

Opposite page. Convenience Foods, clockwise from right hand side; TV Dinner, Chart, page 103; Packaged Lasagna, page 102; and Au Gratin Potatoes, page 102.

Stuffing Mixes

Use instructions on the box. Place water, butter or margarine and seasoning mix in a 2-quart casserole. Cover, bring to a boil and add stuffing mix. Stir and let stand covered for 5 minutes. Cook 1 minute before serving.

Rice Mixes

In 4-quart casserole put 2 cups of water, 2 tablespoons butter or margarine and contents of the seasoning envelope. Bring to a boil, add rice, stir well and cover. Cook 8 minutes, stir, cook 2 minutes and leave covered for 5 minutes. Fluff with fork at serving time.

Au Gratin Potatoes

Empty potato slices into a 2-quart casserole. Sprinkle with cheese sauce mix. Add 2 tablespoons butter or margarine, 2¼ cups boiling water and ⅔ cup of milk. Cover and cook 10 minutes, stirring twice. Remove, raise shelf, preheat infrared browning element 2 minutes, place casserole on shelf and brown for 4 minutes.

Packaged One-dish meals with Vegetables

Brown meat by microwave in 3-quart shallow casserole. Stir often to separate meat. Drain off any fat. Add 3 cups water, seasoning mix and macaroni. Mix well. Cover and cook 8 minutes. Stir frequently. Stir in can of mixed vegetables and heat 2 minutes. Let stand covered for 5 minutes.

V Dinners and Casseroles

ain ourses	Weight	Cooking Container	Microwave Cooking Time	Doneness
/ Dinner eat and tatoes	9-9½ oz.	foil tray *	6-7 min.	Hot
course nner	16 oz.	foil tray *	7 min.	Hot
course nner	16 oz.	foil tray *	8 min.	Hot
oreign inners	16 oz.	foil tray *	6 min.	Hot
ow Calorie	16 oz.	foil tray *	8 min.	Hot
reakfast affle and usage t cake and usage	4½ oz.	foil tray *	2½ min.	Hot
gg and otatoes	4½ oz.	foil tray *	3 min.	Hot
egetable rotein atties and usages esh	8 oz.	wire rack in baking dish	6 min.	Hot
ozen	12 oz.	foil *	7-8 min.	Hot

*Place paper towel under foil tray to protect shelf from arcing damage.

TIPS: Prevent overcooking:
When cooking uneven shapes of meat or those with bones, cover edges with small pieces of foil to prevent overcooking.

If your microwave oven is not a Thermador, follow the manufacturer's instruction for the use of metal.

Vegetables

Very little water is used in cooking vegetables. Therefore there is less chance of losing nutrients in draining. Cook all vegetables covered with the exception of acorn squash, and baked potatoes which are generally cooked whole.

Vegetables should be slightly firm when they are removed from the oven to allow for additional cooking during standing.

Pour the water in the bottom of the dish, add salt to the water, then the vegetables last. If frozen, place ice side up. Cover and cook.

It is best to cook frozen vegetables in a covered casserole, rather than in the package to allow for stirring for even cooking.

Place canned vegetables in a bowl, cover and heat to boiling.

Fresh Corn On The Cob

Fresh corn on the cob should be cooked with the husks and silk intact. By this method they will cook in their own natural moisture. Place on paper towel and turn ears over and rearrange after ½ cooking time.

1 ear	*1½ min.*
2 ears	*3-4 mins.*
3 ears	*5-6 mins.*
4 ears	*7-8 mins.*
6 ears	*8-9 mins.*

When ears are very hot to touch, remove and wrap in kitchen towel or foil. Let stand for at least 5 minutes. Remove husks and silks and serve.

If part of the husk has been cut from the corn as is frequently the case when purchased in the market, place the corn in Brown-in-Bags and seal. It is not necessary to puncture the bags in this instance, as there will not be that much steam formed, because of the short cooking time. Times remain the same as above.

Potatoes

Cooked potatoes, for mashed potatoes or potato salad, should be scrubbed, but not dried. Cut in half, use Brown-in-Bags. 3 potatoes—Place cut potatoes in the bag. Seal with rubber band. Cook 8-9½ mins. or until soft. Let cool in the bag. When cool, pop off the skins. Dice for salad, mash, rice or beat. Add butter and milk as desired. Place mashed potatoes covered in the oven for 30 seconds to reheat just before serving.

Opposite page. Vegetables, clockwise from upper right; Microwave Broiled Tomatoes, page 114; Glazed Carrots, page 112; Stuffed Zucchini, page 116.

vegetables

VEGETABLE	AMOUNT	UTENSIL	METHOD	STIR AND REARRANGE	TIME
Artichokes medium fresh	1	deep bowl covered	1″ of water with 1 garlic clove and 2 tsp. lemon juice. Cook upside down	none	4-4½ mi
	2	deep bowl covered	1″ of water with 1 garlic clove and 2 tsp. lemon juice. Cook upside down	none	6-7 min.
	4	4-qt. casserole covered	1″ of water with 1 garlic clove and 2 tsp. lemon juice. Cook upside down	none	10-11 mi
hearts frozen	10-oz. pkg.	1-qt. covered	2 tbsp. water	stir once	4-5 min.
Asparagus fresh spears	¾ lb.	rectangular baking dish	¼ cup water, add salt to water, then vegetable —cover with plastic wrap	stir once rearrange once	5-6 min.
spears frozen	10 oz.	1-qt. covered	place ice side up	stir twice rearrange once	7-8 min.
cut frozen	9 oz.	1-qt. casserole	slit pouch	stir twice	5-6 min.
Beans frozen, French or cut	10-oz. pkg.	1-qt. covered	2 tbsp. water	stir twice	6-7 min.
Lima	10-oz. pouch	1-qt.	slit pouch	stir once	6-7 min.
	1 lb.	1-qt. covered	½ cup water	stir once	8-10 min
Beets whole	1 bunch 4 to 5 medium	2-qt. covered	cover with water	stir once	12-15 mi
Broccoli fresh	1½ lb. or 1 bunch	2-qt. covered	Quarter the stems to flower. Place stems to outside of dish. ¼ cup water	none	7-9 min.
frozen spears or chopped	10-oz. pkg.	1-qt. covered	place ice side up	stir once	7-8 min.

106

GETABLE	AMOUNT	UTENSIL	METHOD	STIR AND REARRANGE	TIME
ussel routs sh	½ lb.	1-qt. covered	2 tbsp. water	stir once	4-5 min.
zen	10-oz. pkg.	1-qt. covered	2 tbsp. water	stir once	8-9 min.
zen	10-oz. pouch	1-qt. covered	2 tbsp. water	stir once	8-9 min.
rrots sh	2 medium	1-qt. covered	2 tbsp. water	stir once	4-5 min.
ced	4 medium	1-qt. covered	2 tbsp. water	stir once	7-8 min.
	6 medium	1½ qt. covered	2 tbsp. water	stir once	9-10 min.
ed					30 sec. less for each carrot
zen	10-oz. pkg.	1-qt.	place ice side up	stir once	7-8 min.
uliflower sh	1 medium head, whole	1½-qt. covered	2 tbsp. water	none	7-8 min.
	1 medium head, floweretts	1½-qt. covered	2 tbsp. water	stir once	6-7 min.
lery	4 cups cut	1½-qt. covered	2 tbsp. water	stir once	8-10 min.
rn zen	10-oz. pkg.	1-qt. covered	2 tbsp. water, ice side up	stir once	5-6 min.
n on the) frozen	2 ears	covered casserole	no water	——	6-8 min.
	4 ears	covered casserole	no water	——	10-12 min.
ions sh	8 small or 2 large	1-qt. covered	no water	——	6-7 min.
	quartered	1½-qt. covered	no water	——	6-7 min.
zen in am	10-oz. pkg.	1-qt. covered	no water	stir once	5-6 min.
rsnips artered d cored	4 medium	1½-qt. covered	¼ cup water	stir once	7-8 min.

TIPS: Stirring food:

For smooth and even texture of cooked foods, stir at least once to bring outside cooked portions in center and less cooked parts out to edges.

vegetables

VEGETABLE	AMOUNT	UTENSIL	METHOD	STIR AND REARRANGE	TIME
Peas frozen	2 cups	1-qt. covered	2 tbsp. water	stir once	7-8 min.
	3 cups	1½-qt. covered	2 tbsp. water	stir once	9-10 mi
frozen	10-oz. pkg.	1-qt. covered	place ice side up	stir once	5-6 min.
frozen creamed	10-oz. pkg.	1-qt. covered	after defrosted stir until thoroughly mixed	stir twice	5-6 min
Peas and Carrots frozen	10-oz. pkg.	1-qt. covered	place ice side up	stir once	6-7 min.
Potatoes baked fresh	1 medium	place on paper towel	pierce to let steam escape	none	3½-4 m
	2 medium	place on paper towel	pierce, leave 1 inch between		6½-7 m
	3 medium	place on paper towel	pierce, leave 1 inch between		8½-9 m
	4 medium	place on paper towel	pierce, leave 1 inch between		10-11 m
	5 medium	place on paper towel	pierce, leave 1 inch between		13-14 m
	6 medium	place on paper towel	pierce, place in circle; leave 1 inch between		15-16 m
	7 medium	place on paper towel	pierce, place in circle; leave 1 inch between		18-19 m
	8 medium	place on paper towel	pierce, place in circle; leave 1 inch between		21-22 m
Sweet Potatoes yams	1 medium	place on paper towel	pierce	none	3-4 min.
	2 medium	place on paper towel	pierce, leave 1 inch between	none	5-6 min.
	4 medium	place on paper towel	pierce, leave 1 inch between		7-8 min.
	6 medium	place on paper towel	pierce, place in circle, leave 1 inch between		9-10 mi

:GETABLE	AMOUNT	UTENSIL	METHOD	STIR AND REARRANGE	TIME
inach sh	2 bunches	2-qt. covered	cook in water that clings to the leaves from washing	stir twice	5-6 min.
zen f or opped	10-oz. pkg.	1-qt. covered	cook, ice side up	stir twice	6-7 min.
uash orn	1 medium	paper towel	cook whole, then cut, seed and season	none	6-8 min.
	2 medium	paper towel	cook whole, then cut, seed and season		12-14 min.
bbard	6 x 6″ pieces	3-qt. covered	Put 1″ of water in bottom of dish. Place squash skin side up. Remove squash, drain water. Turn squash over, season and cook 1 minute		7-8 min.
zen	10-oz. pkg.	1-qt. covered	season	turn twice	5-6 min.
cchini	2 medium	1-qt. covered	¼ cup water	stir once	6-7 min.
rnips sh ced	4 medium	1½-qt. covered	¼ cup water	stir once	10-12 min.

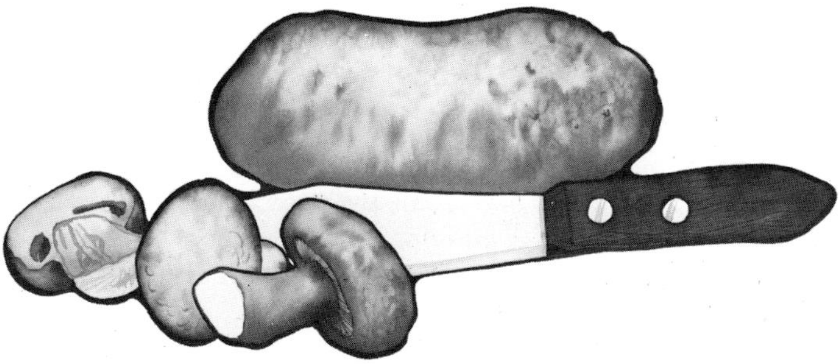

Scalloped Potatoes

4 cups hot water
1 teaspoon salt
4 medium potatoes, peeled and thinly sliced
1 onion, thinly sliced
¼ cup butter or margarine
2 tablespoons flour
1½ cups milk
½ teaspoon seasoned salt
⅛ teaspoon pepper

In 3-quart casserole heat water and salt to boiling by microwave; add potatoes and onion, cover and cook by microwave for 5 minutes, stirring once. Drain. Melt butter in 4-cup glass measure; stir in flour, then milk, seasoned salt and pepper. Cook 3 minutes, or until mixture thickens, stirring every 30 seconds. Place cooked, drained potatoes and onions in 3-quart casserole. Pour sauce over; mix well, cover and cook 6 minutes, stirring once. Let stand, covered for 5 minutes. Makes 4 servings.

**Exact cooking time depends on thickness of potatoes.*

Creamy Cabbage

¼ cup butter
½ small head cabbage, shredded (about 1 quart)
¼ cup light cream
¼ teaspoon salt
¼ teaspoon seasoned salt
⅛ teaspoon pepper

In microwave, melt butter in 2-quart casserole. Add cabbage, stirring to coat with butter. Cover and cook by microwave for 2 minutes. Stir in cream; cover and cook 2 minutes, stir and cook an additional minute. Sprinkle with salt, seasoned salt, and pepper. Let stand several minutes before serving. Makes 4 servings.

Corn Bake

2 (12-ounce) cans whole kernel corn, drained
1 (6-ounce) can evaporated milk
1 egg, beaten slightly
1 tablespoon minced onion
1 tablespoon diced pimento
½ cup shredded Monterey Jack or cheddar cheese
½ teaspoon salt
½ cup soft bread crumbs
1 tablespoon melted butter
¼ cup shredded Monterey Jack or cheddar cheese

Combine corn and milk with egg, onion, pimento, ½ cup cheese and salt. Spoon into 6 x 10-inch baking dish. Toss bread crumbs with butter and remaining ¼ cup cheese. Sprinkle over top, cover with plastic wrap. Cook by microwave for 3 minutes, turn dish and cook another 3 minutes. Let stand 5 minutes. Makes 6 servings.

Harvard Beets

1 (16-ounce) can sliced beets
2 tablespoons sugar
1 tablespoon cornstarch
¼ teaspoon salt
¼ cup vinegar
2 tablespoons butter

Drain beets, reserving ⅓ cup liquid. In small glass bowl, combine sugar, cornstarch, and salt. Mix in vinegar, reserved beet liquid and butter. Cook by microwave for 30 seconds. Stir and cook an additional two and a half minutes or until translucent. Add beets and cook by microwave an additional 30 seconds. Makes 4 servings.

TIPS: Cover foods:
For even distribution of heat and quicker cooking, cover baking dishes with casserole lids, plastic film or waxed paper.

Glazed Carrots

6 carrots, peeled and sliced crosswise
2 tablespoons water
2 tablespoons butter or margarine
¼ cup brown sugar
¼ teaspoon salt
1 teaspoon prepared mustard

Cook carrots in 2 tablespoons water in 1½-quart dish by microwave for 5 minutes. Drain. In 1-cup measuring cup, melt butter by microwave; stir in brown sugar, salt and mustard. Pour over drained carrots. Heat 30 seconds. Makes 4 servings.

Cracker Barrel Beets and Eggs

5 fresh beets
Water
¼ cup brown sugar
½ cup vinegar
½ cup cold water
½ teaspoon salt
1 small stick cinnamon
3 whole cloves
6 hard cooked eggs, peeled

Wash beets. Trim stalks and cover with water in 2-quart casserole. Cook, covered, by microwave for 12 minutes. Let stand, covered, while making sauce. Combine brown sugar with vinegar, cold water, salt, cinnamon and cloves. Drain beets; slip off skins. Pour pickle sauce over beets. Cover and cook 8 minutes by microwave. Let stand several days. Remove beets; add eggs to sauce, cover and let pickle two days in refrigerator before using.

TIPS: Stirring food:
For smooth and even texture of cooked foods, stir at least once to bring outside cooked portions in center and less cooked parts out to edges.

Summer Squash Italiano

3 tablespoons butter or margarine
1 onion, minced
1 clove garlic, minced
1 small green pepper, chopped
4 medium tomatoes, peeled and chopped
½ teaspoon salt
1½ pounds summer squash
½ cup water
1 cup grated Parmesan Cheese

In 2½-quart casserole, melt the butter; add onion, garlic and green pepper. Cook by microwave for about 4 minutes or until vegetables are tender. Add tomatoes and salt; cook 2 minutes, stirring occasionally. Trim stems off squash; cut into slices or cubes. Combine with ½ cup water in 2-quart casserole. Cover and cook by microwave 8 minutes; drain. Arrange alternate layers of half the squash with half the tomato mixture and cheese in 2½-quart casserole. Repeat layers. Cook by microwave 3 minutes. Raise shelf to upper position. Brown under infrared browning element 4 minutes or until it begins to brown. Makes 5 to 6 servings.

Mixed Vegetable Medley

2 (10-ounce) packages frozen, mixed vegetables
¼ teaspoon salt
¼ cup water
3 tablespoons butter
2 tablespoons flour
1 cup light cream or milk
1½ teaspoons instant minced onion

In 2½-quart casserole, combine vegetables with salt and water. Cook, covered, 6 minutes, stirring at least once. Drain and set aside. Melt butter in 2-quart casserole. Blend in flour, then gradually stir in cream or milk. Cook 1 minute; stir and cook 2 minutes longer. Add onion and drained vegetables. Makes 6 servings.

Microwave Broiled Tomatoes

2 medium tomatoes
Salt and pepper
2 tablespoons grated Parmesan cheese
2 tablespoons fine dry bread crumbs
1 tablespoon melted butter or margarine
1 teaspoon chopped chives

Cut tomatoes in half. Sprinkle with salt and pepper. Combine cheese with bread crumbs, butter and chives. Spoon over tomatoes. Place in 9-inch pie plate. Cook by microwave for 30 to 45 seconds. Then raise shelf and brown under infrared browning unit for about 4 minutes. Makes 4 servings.

Glazed Acorn Squash

2 acorn squash
¼ teaspoon grated lemon peel
1 tablespoon lemon juice
¼ teaspoon nutmeg
½ cup honey

Place whole squash on paper towels in microwave; cook 8 to 10 minutes or until soft. Let stand 5 minutes. Slice crosswise into 1-inch slices; scoop out seeds. Combine remaining ingredients. Place squash in 7½ x 12-inch baking dish. Spoon sauce over. Cover and heat by microwave for 2 minutes; turning dish and spooning sauce over squash at least once. Makes 4 servings.

Quickie Baked Beans

4 slices bacon, diced
½ cup chopped onion
1 (28-ounce) can pork and beans
2 tablespoons brown sugar
1 tablespoon Worcestershire sauce
1 teaspoon prepared mustard

In 2½-quart bowl, cook bacon and onion 5 minutes by microwave; drain excess fat. Add beans, brown sugar, Worcestershire and mustard. Cover and cook by microwave for 10 minutes, stirring several times. Makes 5 to 6 servings.

Orange Glazed Sweet Potatoes

3 large, cooked sweet potatoes or 29-ounce can, drained
⅓ cup sugar
1½ teaspoons cornstarch
¼ teaspoon salt
½ teaspoon grated orange peel
½ cup orange juice
2 tablespoons butter or margarine

Peel potatoes, cut into halves. If potatoes are large, cut in quarters. In 4-cup measure, combine sugar with cornstarch. Stir in salt, orange peel and juice. Cook for 2½ minutes, stirring often. Add butter to sauce. Arrange potatoes in 1½-quart baking dish. Pour sauce over and cook in microwave for 3 minutes. Makes 4 to 5 servings.

Scalloped Tomatoes

3 tablespoons butter or margarine
¼ cup minced onion
¼ cup minced celery
1 tablespoon sugar
1 teaspoon salt
2 tablespoons flour
⅛ teaspoon pepper
1 (28-ounce) can tomatoes, cut up
3 slices bread, toasted, buttered and cut into cubes

Melt butter in 1½-quart baking dish; stir in onion and celery; cook by microwave 3 minutes. Add sugar, salt, flour, and pepper; cook 1 minute. Stir in tomatoes. Top with toast cubes. Cook in microwave 5 minutes. Makes 4 servings.

TIPS: Cover foods:
For even distribution of heat and quicker cooking, cover baking dishes with casserole lids, plastic film or waxed paper.

Green Beans Supreme

2 tablespoons butter or margarine
2 tablespoons flour
½ teaspoon salt
1 tablespoon instant minced onion
¼ teaspoon pepper
½ teaspoon grated lemon peel
¼ cup water
1 cup dairy sour cream
2 (16-ounce) cans green beans, drained
¼ cup grated cheddar cheese
2 tablespoons melted butter
½ cup dry bread crumbs

In 4-cup measure or deep bowl, melt 2 tablespoons butter. Stir in flour, salt, onion, pepper, and lemon peel. Cook by microwave for 1 minute. Stir in water, then sour cream. Mix with green beans. Spoon into 1½-quart baking dish. Mix cheese with 2 tablespoons melted butter and bread crumbs. Sprinkle over green beans. Cook by microwave 5 minutes. Makes 6 to 7 servings.

Stuffed Zucchini

4 zucchini
¼ cup water
1 (6-ounce) package chicken flavored stuffing mix
1¾ cups water
¼ cup butter or margarine

In shallow casserole, place whole zucchini with ¼ cup water; cook, covered, 10 to 12 minutes or until tender. Rearrange in dish once. Cool slightlly; cut in half, lengthwise and scoop out centers. In 2-quart bowl combine seasoning packet (from package of stuffing mix) with 1¾ cups water and butter; cook 3 to 4 minutes. Cover and let stand 5 minutes. Stir in crumbs from mix to moisten. Fluff with fork; spoon into cooked zucchini shells. Heat in shallow casserole 1 minute. Makes 8 zucchini shells.

Hot Bean Salad

4 slices bacon
⅓ cup sugar
1 tablespoon cornstarch
1 teaspoon salt
¼ teaspoon pepper
½ cup white wine vinegar
1 onion, sliced
1 (1-pound) can cut green beans, drained
1 (1-pound) can cut wax beans, drained
1 (1-pound) can kidney beans, drained
1 hard cooked egg, sliced

Arrange bacon on rack in 7½ x 12-inch shallow baking dish. Cover with paper towel and cook 2½ minutes or until crisp by microwave. Crumble bacon and set aside. Remove rack; add sugar, cornstarch, salt, pepper, vinegar and onion to drippings in baking dish. Cook 4 to 5 minutes or until thick, stirring several times. Add beans, mixing well. Cover and cook 4 minutes or until beans are hot, stirring once. Sprinkle cooked bacon over top. Garnish with egg. Makes 8 to 9 servings.

Fresh Artichokes

Wash 4 fresh artichokes. Cut stems at base and remove small bottom leaves. Snip off tips of leaves with scissors. Cut 1 inch off top of artichoke. In 4-quart casserole, stand upside down in about 2 inches of water. Add 2 tablespoons lemon juice, 1 teaspoon salt and 1 clove garlic. Cover and cook 11 minutes. Drain; turn artichokes upside down to drain thoroughly, then right side up. Serve with lemon butter or mayonnaise.

TIPS: Seasoning with salt:
Add salt to water when cooking vegetables or at the end of cooking time for meats. Salt draws moisture from food when cooked in microwave oven.

Dilled Zucchini and Mushrooms

4 medium zucchini, cut into 1-inch slices
¼ cup water
⅛ teaspoon dried dill
1 clove garlic
¼ cup butter or margarine
½ pound fresh mushrooms, sliced
2 tablespoons flour
1 cup dairy sour cream
Buttered bread crumbs

In 2-quart shallow casserole, combine zucchini with water, dill, and garlic. Cover and cook 8 minutes, stirring twice during first part of cooking time. Let stand, covered, while making sauce. In 2-quart deep casserole, melt butter or margarine; add mushrooms and cook 2 minutes, stirring often. Stir in flour. Discard garlic clove from zucchini; drain, reserving 2 tablespoons liquid. Add reserve liquid to mushrooms; stir and cook 1 minute. Spoon squash into mushroom mixture; heat 1 minute. Fold in sour cream; sprinkle with crumbs. Raise shelf. Preheat infrared browning element 1 minute. Brown 4 minutes. Makes 5 to 6 servings.

Marie's Tomato Stack-ups

1 (10-ounce) package frozen spinach (drained and chopped)
3 large tomatoes
¼ teaspoon salt
½ cup shredded swiss cheese
¼ cup chopped onion

Put spinach ice side up in 1½-quart casserole. Cook 6 minutes by microwave. After 3 minutes of cooking break up the block of spinach and stir with a fork. Cut the tomatoes in half. Sprinkle lightly with salt. Set aside ¼ cup of the shredded cheese. Combine remaining cheese, spinach, and onion. Place tomato halves in a shallow baking dish. Spoon spinach mixture onto the tomatoes. Cook by microwave for 3 minutes. Raise the shelf to the upper position. Preheat the infrared browning element. Sprinkle the cheese over the spinach. Melt and brown the cheese with infrared browning element for 2 minutes. Serves 6.

Rice with Vegetables

1 cup long-grain rice
2½ cups water
4 tablespoons butter or margarine
½ teaspoon salt
Chop in small pieces:
½ green pepper
2 small tomatoes (discard pulp and seeds)
2 green onions
2 stalks of celery
6 stuffed green olives

Put 1½ cups water, rice, butter or margarine and salt in 4-quart casserole. Cook uncovered for 8 minutes. Stir twice. Add 1 cup of water and cook covered for 5 minutes. With a fork, carefully fluff vegetables into cooked rice and let stand covered for 10 minutes. Serves 4.

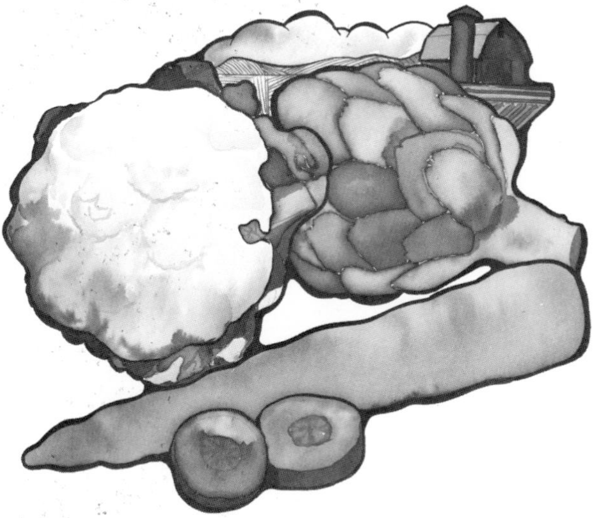

Heating of Bread Items

Fresh or Frozen—It is necessary to operate your oven in this manner when heating these food items that take such a short time (seconds).

Place the food on a paper towel or napkin.

Push the switch to "On", turn the timer dial to 2 or 3 minutes and then back to the number of seconds required, and close the door. Cooking will start at that precise second. If you put the food in the oven, push the "on" switch, close the door and then set the timer, seconds could be added to your cooking time while you are turning the timer.

Overcooking tends to make bread items tough and rubbery in texture.

For instance when hot dogs are cooked right in the buns, the bread is frequently overcooked by the time the hot dog is ready. We suggest they both be placed on a paper plate, heat the bun for 30 seconds, remove it and cook the hot dog an additional 30 seconds, and place the hot dog in the bun.

SUGGESTED HEATING TIMES

1. *Sweet Rolls* — From room temperature heat 15 seconds for the first roll.
   Add 5 seconds for each additional roll.
   From frozen state, heat 20 seconds.
   Add 10 seconds for each additional roll.
2. *Frozen Bread* — Defrost and heat 1 slice for 15 seconds.
   Add 5 seconds for each additional slice.
3. *Frozen Bagel* — Defrost and heat 1 bagel 20 seconds.
   Add 10 seconds for each additional bagel.
4. *Fresh Doughnut* — Heat 1 for 10 seconds.
   Add 5 seconds for each additional doughnut.
5. *Frozen Doughnut* — Defrost and heat 1 doughnut for 25 seconds.
   Add 10 seconds for each additional doughnut.

Opposite page. Bread and Cereals, clockwise from upper center; Popcorn, page 129; Oatmeal, page 126; Bran Muffins, page 122.

Bran Muffins

½ cup bran cereal
½ cup milk
1 tablespoon soft shortening
2 tablespoons molasses
1 egg, beaten
½ cup flour
¼ teaspoon salt
¾ teaspoon baking powder
½ teaspoon baking soda
¼ cup chopped raisins
½ teaspoon grated orange peel

In medium bowl, soak bran in milk for 5 minutes. In the meantime, beat shortening with molasses, add egg and stir until smooth. Stir into softened bran. Add flour, salt, baking powder, soda, raisins and orange peel, stirring until mixed. Spoon into six greased custard cups. Arrange in circle and bake by microwave for 4 to 4½ minutes, turning custard cups once. Makes 6.

Banana Nut Bread

½ cup shortening
¾ cup brown sugar
2 eggs
¾ cup mashed ripe banana
1¼ cups flour
½ teaspoon soda
½ teaspoon baking powder
½ teaspoon salt
¼ cup finely chopped walnuts

Cream shortening and sugar; add eggs and beat well. Add banana alternately with combination of flour, soda, baking powder and salt. Stir in nuts. Pour into wax paper-lined 9 x 5 x 3-inch loaf dish. Cook by microwave for 8 minutes, turning baking dish several times. Let stand at least 10 minutes. Remove from pan; cool on rack.

Cheese Chile Corn Bread

2 eggs
1 (8-ounce) can whole kernel corn
1 tablespoon baking powder
1 cup dairy sour cream
½ cup melted butter or margarine
1 cup corn meal
1 teaspoon salt
½ cup diced green chiles
1 cup grated Jack cheese

Beat eggs; mix with remaining ingredients except chiles and cheese. Pour half the batter into well-greased 8-inch square baking dish. Place chiles on top of batter; sprinkle with half the cheese. Then pour on remaining batter and cheese. Bake by microwave 10 minutes, turning dish one quarter turn three times. Raise shelf. Pre-heat infrared browning unit 2 minutes. Brown for 4 minutes, turning once. Remove from oven and let stand for at least 5 minutes before cutting.

Hot French Herb Bread

½ loaf unsliced French bread
½ cup soft butter or margarine
1 tablespoon Italian herb seasoning
grated Parmesan cheese

Cut bread into 6 thick slices being careful not to cut through the bottom crust. Combine butter with seasoning. Spread between slices; sprinkle cheese on top. Place on paper towels in microwave. Cook 1 to 2 minutes or until hot. Serve immediately. Makes 6 servings.

TIPS: Heat bakery products:
Doughnuts, coffee cakes, muffins and rolls seem freshly baked when heated by microwave. Heat one muffin on paper towel by microwave about 15 seconds.

Make-Your-Own Toasted Cereal

⅓ cup chopped blanched almonds
1 cup quick-cooking rolled oats
⅓ cup wheat germ
⅓ cup raisins
⅓ cup snipped dried apples or apricots
¼ cup brown sugar

Combine almonds, rolled oats and wheat germ. Spread in 7½ x 12-inch baking dish. Raise shelf to top level. Preheat infrared browning unit for 2 minutes. Place baking dish on top shelf. Toast for 3 minutes; stir mixture and brown under infrared element an additional 3 minutes. Remove from heat; stir in raisins, apples or apricots and brown sugar. Store in refrigerator. Serve with milk or cream. Makes about 2½ cups.

Microwave Rice

2 cups hot water
1 cup uncooked regular rice
½ teaspoon salt

Place water in 2½-quart casserole; bring to boil by microwave. Add rice and salt. Cover and cook 5 minutes; stir, cover and cook another 5 minutes. Stir and let stand, covered, several minutes before serving. Makes 4 to 6 servings.

Instant Cream of Wheat

¾ cup water
3 tablespoons instant cream of wheat
⅛ teaspoon salt

In large cereal bowl or 4-cup measure, bring water to boil by microwave. Stir in cream of wheat. Boil 15 seconds. Stir and cover with plastic wrap. Let stand 30 seconds. Add salt and serve. Makes 1 serving.

Regular Cream of Wheat

1¼ cups water
3 tablespoons regular cream of wheat
⅛ teaspoon salt

In 1½-quart bowl, bring water to boil by microwave. Stir in cereal. Cook 3 minutes, stirring once every minute. Cover and let stand 1 minute. Add salt. Makes 1 serving.

Regular Cream of Wheat (4 servings)

3¾ cups water
½ teaspoon salt
⅔ cups regular cream of wheat

Bring water and salt to boil in 3-quart bowl. Stir in cereal. Cook 30 seconds and stir. Cook another 3 minutes, stirring once every minute. Cover; let stand 2 minutes. Makes 4 servings.

Quick Cream of Wheat

1 cup water
3 tablespoons quick cream of wheat
⅛ teaspoon salt

In large cereal bowl or 4-cup measure, bring water to boil by microwave. Stir in cream of wheat; cook 1 minute, 30 seconds; stirring every 30 seconds. Cover and let stand 1 minute. Add salt. Makes 1 serving.

TIPS: Stirring food:
For smooth and even texture of cooked foods, stir at least once to bring outside cooked portions in center and less cooked parts out to edges.

Quick Cooking Oatmeal

¾ cup water
⅓ cup quick cooking oats
¼ teaspoon salt

In large cereal bowl or 4-cup measure, heat water to boil by microwave. Stir in oats. Cover with plastic wrap and cook 15 seconds. Let stand, covered, 1 minute. Stir in salt and serve. Makes 1 serving.

Quick Cooking Oatmeal (4 servings)

3 cups water
½ teaspoon salt
1⅓ cups quick cooking oats

In 3-quart casserole, bring water and salt to boil. Stir in oats. Cover and cook 1 minute. Let stand, covered for 2 minutes. Makes 4 servings.

Old Fashioned Oatmeal

1 cup water
⅓ cup regular oats
¼ teaspoon salt

In large cereal bowl, heat water to boil by microwave. Stir in oats; cook 1 minute. Stir; cover and cook 1 minute. Let stand another minute. Add salt and serve. Makes 1 serving.

TIPS: Rotate position of baking dishes:
For quick and even cooking, remember to rotate dishes at least once while cooking by microwave.

Wheat Hearts

1 cup water
¼ cup wheat hearts
¼ teaspoon salt

In cereal bowl, bring water to boil by microwave. Stir in wheat hearts. Cook by microwave 30 seconds; stir and cook another 30 seconds. Stir well and serve. Makes 1 serving.

Wheat Hearts (4 servings)

4 cups water
1 teaspoon salt
1 cup wheat hearts

In 3-quart bowl, bring water and salt to boil by microwave. Stir in wheat hearts. Cook by microwave 30 seconds; stir. Cook 1 minute; stir. Cook 30 seconds. Cover and let stand 1 minute. Makes 4 servings.

Streusel Coffee Cake

⅓ cup brown sugar, packed
⅓ cup chopped nuts
1 teaspoon cinnamon
½ (18.5-ounce) package yellow cake mix

Mix brown sugar, nuts and cinnamon; set aside. Prepare cake mix according to package directions. Pour ½ of batter into waxed paper lined round 8¼-inch or 8-inch square baking dish. Sprinkle with ½ the streusel mixture. Repeat with remaining batter and topping. Cook by microwave 6½ minutes, turning dish several times. Let stand at least 5 minutes. Cut into wedges or squares.

Sour Cream Coffee Cake

½ cup butter or margarine
1 cup sugar
3 eggs
1 teaspoon vanilla
Sift together:
1½ cups cake flour
½ cup all purpose flour
1 teaspoon baking powder
1 teaspoon baking soda

½ pint Hampshire sour cream

Cream butter or margarine and sugar together. Beat in eggs, add vanilla. Fold in flour and sour cream alternately. Flour should be added first and last. Line the bottom of 2 - 8¼-inch baking dishes with 2 layers of waxed paper. Put ¼ of the batter in each cake dish. Sprinkle each with ¼ of the topping. Spread the remainder of the batter over each cake. Use icing knife to spread batter. Sprinkle with remaining topping. Let batter stand for 15 minutes. Place a sheet of waxed paper over each layer. Bake each layer by microwave for 4 minutes with shelf in upper position. Let cakes cool in dishes 5 minutes before turning onto cooling rack.

Topping

¾ cup brown sugar firmly packed
¼ cup soft butter or margarine
4 tablespoons flour
¼ teaspoon salt
¼ teaspoon cinnamon
¼ cup chopped nuts

Cut ingredients together with pastry blender. Then add nuts.

Corn Popping

Use a 2-quart oven-proof dish with knob cover. The dish and knob get very hot so use hot pads.

2 tablespoons vegetable oil
⅓ cup popcorn

Put 2 tablespoons oil in dish. Preheat this oil only for the first batch of corn. Add ⅓ cup popcorn and cook the first batch of corn 5 minutes. The following batches will only take 4 minutes to pop.

Always remove popcorn from covered dish as soon as it is popped or husks will turn black. Always place the dish on bread board when adding more oil and popcorn. Placing it on a cold surface could crack or break it.

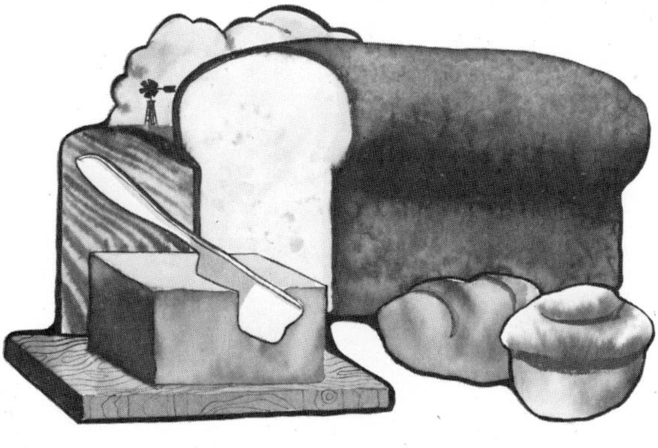

S'Mores

8 graham crackers
4 large marshmallows
1 (1.05-ounce) milk chocolate candy bar

Make 4 sandwiches of graham crackers with marshmallows and chocolate bar as filling. Place on paper plates; cover with paper towel. Heat by microwave for 15 to 20 seconds or until marshmallow melts. Makes 4.

Merry Mints

3 tablespoons butter or margarine
3 tablespoons milk
1 (15.4-ounce) package creamy white frosting mix
½ teaspoon peppermint extract
Food coloring

In 1½-quart bowl heat butter and milk until butter melts. Stir in frosting mix. Cook by microwave 1½ to 2 minutes or until bubbly. Stir often. Add peppermint and desired food coloring. Drop from spoon on waxed paper. Makes about 4 dozen.

Fudgie Scotch Wedges

1½ cups graham cracker crumbs
½ package (½-cup) semi-sweet chocolate bits
1 package (1-cup) butterscotch bits
1 cup coarsely chopped walnuts
1 can sweetened condensed milk

Mix dry ingredients. Stir in condensed milk; mix well. Grease an 8-inch round baking dish. Invert a shot glass (1-oz.) in center of dish. Spoon the mixture into the dish around the glass. Cook by microwave 6 minutes; turn the dish twice. Remove dish and raise shelf to upper position. Preheat infrared browning element 2 minutes. Brown wedges 3 to 3½ minutes, turning at least once. Cool for 30 minutes. Remove glass from center; cut into small wedges and serve. Makes about 16 pieces.

Opposite page. Confections, clockwise upper left; Divinity, page 133; Merry Mints, page 131; Fantastic Fudge, page 133.

Spiced Nuts

1½ cups sugar
½ cup orange juice
¼ teaspoon cinnamon
⅛ teaspoon nutmeg
2½ cups shelled walnuts or pecans

In 3-quart casserole, cook sugar and orange juice by microwave for 7½ minutes or until soft ball stage, stirring several times. Remove from microwave; add spices and nuts. Stir until mixture begins to look cloudy. Drop by spoonfuls on waxed paper. Separate into small clusters or individual nuts.

Peanut Crunchies

¼ cup butter or margarine
½ cup chunk-style peanut butter
½ pound marshmallows
2 (1-ounce each) squares unsweetened chocolate
3 cups sugar-coated corn flakes

Combine butter, peanut butter, marshmallows, and chocolate in 3-quart casserole. Cook 4 minutes (or until ingredients are melted) by microwave stirring often. Remove from microwave. Add corn flakes and mix well. Pack into buttered 8-inch square baking dish. Chill until set. Cut into 28 bars.

TIPS: Melt marshmallows:
Marshmallows melt almost instantly by microwave.

Fantastic Fudge

4 cups sugar
1 (14-ounce) can evaporated milk
1 cup butter or margarine
1 (12-ounce) semi-sweet chocolate pieces
1 (7-ounce) jar marshmallow creme
1 teaspoon vanilla
1 cup chopped walnuts

In 4-quart bowl, combine sugar, milk and butter. Cook by microwave 18 to 20 minutes or until mixture reaches soft ball stage. Stir often while mixture is cooking. Watch carefully to avoid a boil-over. Mix in chocolate and marshmallow creme. Stir until well blended. Add vanilla and nuts. Pour into buttered 9-inch square dish for thick pieces. For thinner ones, use 7½ x 12-inch dish. Cool and cut into squares. Makes about 20 pieces.

Divinity

3 cups granulated sugar
½ cup light corn syrup
⅔ cup water
¼ teaspoon salt
2 egg whites
¼ teaspoon vanilla
1 cup chopped nuts

In 3-quart bowl cook sugar, syrup and water 12 minutes 15 seconds (should spin a fine thread). Add salt to egg whites and beat them on high speed until stiff. Slowly pour syrup in a thin stream into the egg whites, beating constantly until mixture loses its shine and thickens. Stir in vanilla and nuts. Drop by teaspoons at once on waxed paper. Makes about 30 pieces.

Pecan Pralines

1 cup granulated sugar
2 cups firmly packed brown sugar
¼ cup light corn syrup
⅛ teaspoon salt
1¼ cups milk
1 teaspoon vanilla
1½ cups pecan halves

Combine sugars, corn syrup, salt and milk in 4-quart casserole. Cook by microwave 13 to 13½ minutes or until a little of mixture dropped into cold water forms a soft ball. Stir often while cooking. Beat until mixture begins to thicken. Stir in vanilla and pecans. Drop from tablespoon on waxed paper and spread to form patties about 3 inches in diameter. Let stand until firm. Makes about 16 to 18 pralines.

Chinese Chews

1 (6-ounce) package chocolate chips
1 (6-ounce) package butterscotch chips
1 (3-ounce) can chow mein noodles
1 (6½-ounce) can cocktail peanuts

Place the chocolate and butterscotch chips in a 2-quart casserole. Melt 2 minutes by microwave. Stir until smooth. Add peanuts and chow mein noodles. Stir until well coated. Drop by teaspoon onto waxed paper-lined tray. Let set in refrigerator until firm. Yield: 4 dozen.

Opposite page. Desserts; Fresh Strawberry Pie, page 149.

Old Fashioned Bread Pudding

2 cups milk
1 tablespoon butter or margarine
3 eggs
½ cup sugar
¼ teaspoon salt
1 teaspoon vanilla
½ teaspoon cinnamon
½ cup raisins
3 cups soft bread cubes

In 4-cup glass measuring cup, heat milk and butter by microwave for 3 minutes. Beat eggs; blend in sugar. Gradually add hot milk to eggs, stir until well blended. Stir in salt, vanilla, cinnamon and raisins. Place bread in 10 x 6-inch baking dish. Pour egg mixture over bread. Cook 3 minutes by microwave; turn and cook another 2 minutes. Raise shelf. Pre-heat infrared browning unit for 2 minutes. Brown for 4 minutes. Makes 6 servings.

Chewy Nut Bars

3 tablespoons butter or margarine
½ cup flour
¼ teaspoon baking soda
⅛ teaspoon salt
1½ cups brown sugar
1½ cups finely chopped walnuts
3 beaten eggs
1½ teaspoon vanilla
Powdered sugar

In 7½ x 12-inch baking dish, melt butter by microwave. In mixing bowl, combine flour, soda, salt, brown sugar, and nuts. Stir in eggs and vanilla. Carefully pour batter over melted butter in baking dish. Do not stir. Cook by microwave for 4 minutes. Turn dish; cook another 4 minutes. Remove from microwave. Raise shelf and preheat infrared browning unit 1 minute. Brown with browning unit for 1 minute. Sprinkle with powdered sugar. Place waxed paper under wire rack. Invert baking dish immediately onto rack; cool. Sprinkle again with powdered sugar. Cut into bars. Makes about 24 bars.

Chunky Applesauce

6 cooking apples
1/3 cup water
1/3 cup sugar

Peel and core apples. Cut into small chunks. In 3-quart casserole, combine apples with water. Cover and cook by microwave 8 minutes, stirring several times. Add sugar and cook an additional 2 minutes. Let stand, covered for 5 minutes. Cool; sprinkle with nutmeg or cinnamon, if desired. Makes about 2 cups.

Pie Crust

Use your favorite recipe for pie crust. Mix and roll out as usual. For single crust pie, fit pastry into 9-inch pie plate. Build up and crimp edges. Cut waxed paper into 11-inch circle; slash edges 1½-inches deep around sides. Fit 8-inch pie plate on waxed paper. Cook by microwave 3 minutes. Remove 8-inch pie plate and waxed paper; cook 3 minutes longer. Leave shelf in bottom position; brown crust under infrared browning unit for 5 minutes, turning several times. Cool and fill.

Lemon Pie Filling

1½ cups sugar
1/3 cup cornstarch
1½ cups boiling water
3 egg yolks, slightly beaten
1/3 cup lemon juice
1 tablespoon lemon peel
3 tablespoons butter
1 baked 9-inch pastry shell

Mix sugar and cornstarch together in 1½-quart glass bowl. Add boiling water and cook 2 minutes; stir with wisk. Cook 2 or 2½ minutes longer or until translucent; stir again. Gradually add some of hot mixture to beaten egg yolks. Then add to remaining hot mixture. Mix well; cook 45 seconds. Stir in lemon juice, peel and butter. Pour into baked pie crust. Cool; top with whipped cream or meringue.

Grasshopper Pie

32 to 35 small chocolate cookies (about 4 ounces)
35 large marshmallows (about 8 ounces)
½ cup milk
¼ cup green creme de menthe
¼ cup white creme de cacao
Several drops green food coloring
1 cup whipping cream
Whipped cream for garnish
Chocolate curls

Line bottom and sides of 9-inch pie plate with cookies. In 2-quart bowl, heat marshmallows and milk by microwave for 2 minutes to 2 minutes and 15 seconds, or until marshmallows are puffy and begin to melt. Stir well until marshmallows are completely melted. Cool several minutes. Stir in liqueurs and food coloring. Cool until partially thickened. Whip cream; fold into marshmallow mixture. Spoon into cookie-lined pie plate. Refrigerate until firm. Garnish with additional whipped cream and chocolate curls if desired.

Pumpkin Pie

1½ cups canned pumpkin
1 cup evaporated milk
2 eggs, beaten slightly
¾ cup sugar
¼ teaspoon salt
½ teaspoon cinnamon
½ teaspoon nutmeg
1 (9-inch) baked pie shell
1 tablespoon flour

In 1½-quart bowl, combine pumpkin and evaporated milk. Cook by microwave for 5 minutes. Mix eggs with sugar, salt, cinnamon and nutmeg. Add hot pumpkin mixture to eggs. Stir well and pour into baked pie shell that has been sprinkled with flour. Cook by microwave, with shelf in upper position, for 5 minutes. Brown with infrared browning unit 5 minutes. Center of pie will still be soft. Cool.

Banana Split Topping

2 tablespoons butter or margarine
2 firm bananas (with slightly green tips)
1 teaspoon lemon juice
¼ cup brown sugar
⅛ teaspoon rum flavoring or 1 tablespoon rum

In 8-inch square baking dish, melt butter by microwave. Cut bananas lengthwise in half, then crosswise in half. Place, cut side down in melted butter. Sprinkle with lemon juice; then brown sugar and rum. Cook by microwave for 30 seconds; rearrange bananas in dish and cook another 30 to 45 seconds. Serve warm over vanilla or butter pecan ice cream.

Deluxe Strawberry Shortcake

2½ cups packaged biscuit mix
¼ cup sugar
1 egg, beaten slightly
½ cup milk
2 tablespoons melted butter or margarine
¼ cup sugar
4 cups fresh sliced strawberries
1 cup whipping cream

Combine biscuit mix with sugar. Add egg to milk and butter, then stir into biscuit mix with a fork. Pat into ungreased, round 8-inch baking dish. Cook by microwave 3 minutes, turn pan half turn and cook an additional 1½ minutes. Remove from microwave. Raise shelf. Preheat infrared browning unit 1 minute. Brown 1½ to 2 minutes. Let stand 5 minutes. In the meantime, add sugar to strawberries. When shortcake is cool, split horizontally. Whip cream. Spoon sweetened berries and whipped cream between layers and over top. If desired, save a few whole berries for the top. Makes 5 to 6 servings.

TIPS: Use measuring cups for shortcuts:
Save dishwashing and time by using 2 or 4 cup glass measuring cups for heating leftovers, making sauces, and melting butter.

German Chocolate Frosting

1 cup evaporated milk
1 cup sugar
3 egg yolks, beaten slightly
¼ cup butter or margarine
1 teaspoon vanilla
1⅓ cups flaked coconut
1 cup chopped pecans

In deep 2-quart glass bowl, combine milk, sugar, egg yolks, butter or margarine and vanilla. Cook by microwave 4½ minutes, stirring often. Cool; beat until thick and shiny. Stir in coconut and pecans. Spread between layers and on top of cake.

Double Duty Cake Mix

1 package cake mix (yellow, white, spice, chocolate, etc.)
2 eggs
1⅓ or 1½ cups water

Pour cake mix into mixing bowl; add eggs and water. Beat according to package directions. Fill 6 paper-lined custard cups half full. Line bottom of 7½ x 12-inch baking dish with waxed paper. Spoon remainder of batter into baking dish. Let batter stand for 15 minutes. Bake cup cakes for 1 minute, 30 seconds on lower shelf. Remove from microwave. Then bake rectangular cake for 7 minutes on lower shelf. Raise shelf. Preheat infrared browning unit for 2 minutes; brown rectangular cake for 3 minutes. Cool. Top with Brown 'n Serve Peanut Butter Frosting.

Brown 'n Serve Peanut Butter Frosting

¼ cup peanut butter
¼ cup light cream
1 cup brown sugar
1 baked (7½ x 12-inch) yellow or chocolate cake

Mix peanut butter with cream and sugar. Spoon on cooled cake. Preheat infrared browning unit 2 minutes. Brown for 1 minute. Turn and brown another 1½ minutes or until bubbly and slightly brown.

Cherry Cobbler

1 (21-ounce) can prepared cherry pie filling
¾ cup flour
2 tablespoons sugar
1 teaspoon baking powder
⅛ teaspoon salt
3 tablespoons butter or margarine, softened
2 tablespoons milk
1 egg, beaten slightly

Pour pie filling into 8¼-inch shallow round baking dish. Combine flour with sugar, baking powder and salt. Cut in butter until mixture resembles coarse crumbs. Mix milk with egg. Add to dry mixture, stirring just to moisten. Spoon topping over fruit in 5 mounds. Cook by microwave for 6 minutes turning baking dish several times. Raise shelf; brown cobbler on upper shelf, under infrared browning unit for 4 minutes, turning dish several times. Makes 5 servings.

Baked Apples

5 medium cooking apples
3 tablespoons butter or margarine
⅓ cup brown sugar
¼ cup chopped dates or raisins (optional)
cinnamon or nutmeg

Core apples; cut a strip of peel from top of each. Place in 8¼-inch shallow round baking dish. Dot with butter; sprinkle tops with sugar. Fill centers with dates or raisins, if desired. Sprinkle with cinnamon or nutmeg. Cook by microwave oven for 6 minutes*, turning apples in dish once. Let stand several minutes. Serve warm or cold.

**Cooking time will vary with the size and variety of apple. Also, allow about 1 minute additional cooking time if apples are filled with dates or raisins.*

German Chocolate Cake

1 (4-ounce) bar sweet cooking chocolate
⅓ cup water
½ cup butter or margarine
1 cup sugar
3 eggs
1 teaspoon vanilla
1¾ cups flour
1 teaspoon soda
½ teaspoon salt
⅔ cup buttermilk

Combine chocolate with water in 2-cup measure; cook by microwave for 2 minutes, stirring several times; cool. Cream butter; gradually add sugar, creaming until light. Add eggs, one at a time, beating well after each. Blend in vanilla and chocolate mixture. Sift together dry ingredients. Add to creamed mixture, alternately with buttermilk, beating after each addition. Line bottom of 2 - 8¼-inch baking dishes with 2 layers of waxed paper. Pour in batter. Let stand 15 minutes. Cook, one layer at a time, by microwave for 4 minutes. Cool 5 minutes; turn out on cooling rack.

Rocky Road Frosting

2 (1-ounce) squares unsweetened chocolate
1 cup miniature marshmallows
¼ cup water
¼ cup butter or margarine
2 cups sifted powdered sugar
1 teaspoon vanilla
1 cup miniature marshmallows
½ cup chopped pecans

In 1½-quart bowl, combine chocolate, 1 cup marshmallows, water and butter. Cook by microwave 1 minute and 15 seconds or until marshmallows melt; stir once. Cool slightly. Add sugar and vanilla; beat until smooth and thick enough to spread. Stir in remaining 1 cup marshmallows and nuts. Makes enough to frost between layers and on top of 8 or 9-inch layer cake, or for top of 7½ x 12-inch cake.

Creamy Cheese Pie

Crust:
1 cup graham cracker crumbs
¼ cup melted butter or margarine

Filling:
2 well beaten eggs
1 (8-ounce) package cream cheese, softened
½ cup sugar
⅛ teaspoon salt
1 teaspoon vanilla
⅛ teaspoon almond flavoring
1½ cups dairy sour cream
cinnamon

Mix graham cracker crumbs with butter. Press on sides and bottom of 9-inch pie plate. In mixing bowl, combine eggs with cream cheese, sugar, salt, vanilla and almond. Beat until smooth. Stir in sour cream. Pour into crumb crust. Raise shelf of microwave to upper level. Cook cheesecake on upper shelf by microwave for 7 minutes, turning dish a quarter turn every two minutes. Cool thoroughly. Serve plain or sprinkle with cinnamon or top with prepared fruit pie filling.

Elegant Chocolate Frosting

1¼ cups sugar
1 cup evaporated milk or heavy cream
5 squares (5-ounces) unsweetened chocolate
½ cup butter or margarine
1 teaspoon vanilla

Mix sugar and milk in deep 1½-quart glass bowl. Cook by microwave 4½ minutes, stirring often. Remove from heat. Add chocolate; stir to blend. Add butter and vanilla. Chill until mixture begins to thicken. Beat until creamy and shiny. Makes enough to fill and frost 8-inch layer cake.

Apple Crumble

5 cooking apples, peeled and sliced
½ teaspoon cinnamon
¼ teaspoon nutmeg
1 teaspoon lemon juice
¼ cup butter or margarine
½ cup brown sugar
¼ cup flour

Mix apples with cinnamon, nutmeg and lemon juice. Place in 8¼-inch round baking dish. With pastry blender, cut butter into sugar and flour. Sprinkle on apples. Cook by microwave for 6 minutes. Turn baking dish and cook another 4 minutes. Let stand at least 5 minutes. Serve warm with cream or ice cream. Makes 4 to 5 servings.

Dream Bars

½ cup (1 stick) butter or margarine
½ cup brown sugar, firmly packed
1 cup flour
2 eggs
1 cup brown sugar, firmly packed
1 teaspoon vanilla
2 tablespoons flour
½ teaspoon salt
½ teaspoon baking powder
1⅓ cups flaked coconut (3½-ounce can)
¾ cup chopped nuts

Cut butter into ½ cup brown sugar and 1 cup flour with pastry blender or fork. Pat into 7½ x 12-inch baking dish. Cook by microwave for 3 minutes. Beat eggs with 1 cup brown sugar and vanilla. Combine 2 tablespoons flour with salt and baking powder. Toss together with coconut and nuts. Stir into egg mixture. Pour over cooked crust. Cook by microwave for 5 minutes. Remove from oven. Raise shelf. Turn on infrared browning unit; brown for 1 minute. Cool slightly; cut into bars. Serve plain or frosted. Makes 24 bars.

Baked Custard

2 cups milk
3 eggs, beaten slightly
¼ cup sugar
½ teaspoon vanilla
Nutmeg

In 4-cup glass measure, heat milk by microwave for 3 minutes. Add eggs, sugar and vanilla with rotary beater. Pour into 5 (6-ounce) custard cups. Sprinkle with nutmeg. Arrange in circle 1 inch apart. Cook for 2½ minutes by microwave. Rearrange custard cups on shelf; let stand for 45 seconds. Cook 2½ minutes longer. Cool. Makes 5 servings.

Seven Minute Frosting

1½ cups sugar
¼ teaspoon cream of tartar
6 tablespoons water
3 egg whites

Cook sugar, cream of tartar and water in 1-quart measuring cup for 4½ minutes. Stir after 2 minutes of cooking time. Beat 3 egg whites to the soft peak stage. Slowly add the syrup (with beaters on high speed) until icing is thick. If icing gets too thick and has a tendency to break or crumble cake, cook for 10 seconds by microwave to soften.

TIPS: For top browning of food:
For browning, be sure to raise shelf to upper level and push button labeled "infrared". Microwave indicator light will be out.

Peach Melba

1 package frozen raspberries
½ cup currant jelly
2 tablespoons cornstarch
2 tablespoons water
6 canned peach halves
Vanilla ice cream

Place the raspberries in 1½-quart glass bowl. Thaw by microwave for 3 minutes. Mash berries with a spoon. Sieve to separate the seeds. Add the jelly and just bring to a boil. Add the cornstarch mixed with water and cook until clear and mixture thickens, stirring often with wire whip. Chill. Place a canned peach half, cut side up, in each individual dessert dish. Top each with scoop of ice cream and pour the cooled sauce over the top. Serves 6.

Golden Carrot Cake

1½ cups flour
1 cup sugar
1 teaspoon baking powder
1 teaspoon soda
½ teaspoon cinnamon
½ teaspoon salt
⅔ cup salad oil
2 eggs
1 cup finely shredded carrot
½ cup crushed pineapple (not drained)
1 teaspoon vanilla
½ cup finely chopped pecans

Sift together flour, sugar, baking powder, soda, cinnamon and salt. Add oil, eggs, carrot, pineapple and vanilla. Mix until all ingredients are moistened. Beat with electric mixer at medium speed for 2 minutes. Stir in pecans. Pour into waxed paper-lined 7½ x 12-inch baking dish. Cook by microwave 4 minutes. Turn baking dish ½ turn; cook another 3 minutes. Remove from oven. Raise shelf. Brown cake on upper level with infrared browning unit for 1½ minutes.

Brownies

½ cup butter or margarine
1 cup sugar
1 teaspoon vanilla
2 eggs
2 (1-ounce) squares unsweetened chocolate
½ cup flour
½ cup chopped walnuts

Cream butter and sugar. Beat in vanilla, then eggs. In 1-cup glass measuring cup, melt chocolate by microwave. Add to egg mixture. Stir in flour and nuts. Pour into waxed paper-lined 8-inch square baking dish. Cook by microwave for 3 minutes; turn dish and cook another 3 minutes. Let stand 5 minutes. Serve plain or with chocolate frosting. Makes 16 pieces.

Quick Peach Brulee

2 fresh peaches, peeled and halved or 4 canned peach halves, drained
¾ cup dairy sour cream
1 tablespoon granulated sugar
¼ teaspoon grated lemon peel
¾ cup brown sugar

Arrange peach halves, cut side down, in 4 custard cups. Cook by microwave 1 minute. Combine sour cream with granulated sugar and lemon peel. Spoon over fruit. Just before serving, sprinkle brown sugar over entire surface of sour cream. Raise shelf in microwave. Brown desserts under infrared browning unit for 3 to 3½ minutes or until brown sugar begins to melt. Serve immediately. Makes 4 servings.

TIPS: ***Soften butter and cream cheese:***
Soften one stick of butter or 1 (3-ounce) package of cream cheese for 5 seconds in microwave.

Meringue

3 egg whites
⅛ teaspoon salt
6 tablespoons sugar

Beat egg whites with salt until frothy. Gradually beat in sugar. Beat until stiff and glossy. Spread over cooked filling (such as lemon, coconut, chocolate or butterscotch) in 9-inch pie. Seal meringue to edge of crust to prevent shrinkage. Cook on bottom shelf of microwave for 2½ minutes, turning several times. With infrared browning unit, brown on lower shelf for about 4 minutes, turning several times.

Packaged Egg Custard

1 (3-ounce) package egg custard mix
2 cups milk
Nutmeg

In 4-cup measure or 1½-quart deep bowl, combine custard mix with milk. Cook by microwave for about 4½ to 5 minutes or until mixture boils, stirring often. Pour into four custard cups or dessert dishes. Sprinkle with nutmeg. Cool until firm. Makes 4 servings.

Packaged Pudding and Pie Filling

1 (3¼-ounce) package pudding and pie filling
2 cups milk

In 4-cup measure mix pudding with milk. Cook by microwave for 4½ to 5 minutes or until mixture boils, stirring often. Cover with plastic wrap and cool. Makes 4 servings.

TIPS: Melt butter:
Melt 2 tablespoons butter in 15 seconds; ¼ cup in 30 seconds in glass measuring cup.

Fresh Strawberry Pie

5 cups fresh strawberries
1 cup water
¾ cup sugar
3 tablespoons cornstarch
Red food coloring
1 (9-inch) cooked pastry shell, cooled

Crush 1 cup of the smaller berries. In 4-cup measure, combine small crushed berries with water; cook by microwave 4 minutes, stirring once. Sieve and return to 4-cup measure. Combine sugar and cornstarch; stir into strawberry juice. Cook by microwave 2 or 3 minutes or until translucent, stirring often. Add several drops food coloring. Place remaining whole berries in baked pie shell; pour glaze over and chill. Serve plain or with whipped cream.

Pineapple Upside Down Cake

2 tablespoons butter or margarine
½ cup brown sugar, firmly packed
5 slices pineapple with syrup
5 maraschino cherries
*½ (18.5 ounce) package yellow cake mix**

Melt butter in 8¼-inch round or 8-inch square dish in microwave. Stir in brown sugar. Drain pineapple, reserving syrup. Arrange pineapple slices and cherries over brown sugar. Prepare cake mix according to package directions, substituting pineapple syrup for water. Spoon batter over pineapple. Cook by microwave 5 or 6 minutes, turning dish several times. Let stand 1 minute. Turn upside down on cake plate. Serve warm or cold.

**Use other half for another upside down cake or for cupcakes.*

Apple Pie

Dough for double-crust pie, (page 137)
8 pippin apples cored, peeled and sliced
1½ cups sugar
4 tablespoons flour
½ teaspoon cinnamon
½ teaspoon salt
½ teaspoon nutmeg
1 tablespoon flour

Toss the apples in the sugar, flour, cinnamon and nutmeg mixture until well coated. Make and bake the bottom crust as directed for a microwave single-crust pie. Sprinkle a tablespoon of flour on the baked crust. Place apples in the pie shell. Do not mound, but place apples so the top of the pie will be even with edge of the shell. Roll out the dough for the top crust and cut to the size of an inverted 9-inch pie plate. Cut a design in the top crust for steam vents. Brush with cream and sprinkle with sugar. Fold the crust in the center. Pick up crust and place over the apples. Put shelf in upper position. Preheat infrared browning element for a minute. Brown crust for 3 to 4 minutes. Lower the shelf and cook the pie for 9 minutes by microwave.

Richard Deacon's Bitter and Booze

1 (6-ounce) package of semi-sweet chocolate chips
½ pint whipping cream
2 jiggers of brandy
¼ teaspoon salt

Melt the chocolate chips in a 1-cup measure for 1½ minutes by microwave. Beat until smooth. Set aside to cool. Whip the cream until stiff. Fold in the brandy, salt and chocolate. Spoon into dessert glasses and chill in the refrigerator.

Sweet Potato Pie

1 (5⅓-ounce) can of evaporated milk
½ cup butter or margarine
1 (1-pound 13-ounce) can sweet potatoes drained and mashed
4 eggs, slightly beaten
1 cup sugar
½ teaspoon salt
1 teaspoon nutmeg
½ teaspoon mace
1 (9-inch) baked pie shell

Cook milk, butter or margarine and sweet potatoes in 1½-quart bowl for 5 minutes, stirring often. Beat with electric mixer or blender until smooth. Add the slightly beaten eggs to the sugar and spices. Add the hot mixture to the egg mixture. Stir well and pour into baked pie shell (which has been sprinkled with 1 tablespoon of flour). Move shelf to upper position. Cook 5 minutes by microwave. Brown with infrared browning element 5 minutes. Cool.

While none of the recipes in this book use the browning dish, Thermador does have such a dish available as an accessory. Recipes for its use are included with the dish.

A set of special cookware is also available. This set includes the utility dish with the metal rack described frequently in this book.

A

B

B *(continued)*

C

C *(continued)*

C *(continued)*

D

E

F

S (continued)

T

U

V

W

Z

notes

notes

notes